M000217033

Helen McIntosh is a wise, lovely, godly woman. In this book, she will lead you through the process of discovering the beauty of life with God at the center.

—*Kay Arthur, cofounder of Precept Ministries International, a four-time Gold Medallion winner, and the author of many books, including* Lord, Heal My Hurts *and* As Silver Refined: Learning to Embrace Life's Disappointments

Jesus cautioned us about becoming Outer Cup People. Dr. McIntosh provides a path to becoming an inner-person, healing from the inside out.

—*Steve Arterburn, director of New Life Ministries and Women of Faith tours, and bestselling author, whose books include* Every Man's Battle *and* Healing is a Choice

Dr. McIntosh's personal warmth and caring flows from every page as she gives tangible ways to help women overcome negative patterns of thinking.

—*Stasi Eldredge, bestselling co-author of* Captivating

How we think affects how we live and how we relate to one another, but few of us know how to separate the truth from what we feel. In this honest, insightful book, Dr. McIntosh gives us tools to help us live and love and pass on godly, healing habits to our children.

—*Sheila Walsh, bestselling author of* Honestly, Extraordinary Faith, *and* The Heartache No One Sees

Dr. McIntosh gives us a wise, insightful book to help change painful thought patterns and damaging self-talk. I recommend this book to anyone who wants to challenge faulty thinking.

—*Jan Silvious, author of* Big Girls Don't Whine, Look at It This Way, *and* Foolproofing Your Life

Everyone who reads this book will benefit from Helen's step-by-step solutions, her sample dialogues, and the spiritual focus it delivers.

—*June Hunt, author, singer, and founder of* Hope for the Heart, *a radio ministry heard daily around the world*

MESSAGES
to MYSELF

Overcoming a Distorted Self-Image

Helen B. McIntosh

BEACON HILL PRESS
OF KANSAS CITY

Copyright 2009
by Helen B. McIntosh and Beacon Hill Press of Kansas City

ISBN 978-0-8341-2456-1

Printed in the United States of America

Cover Design: Darlene Filley
Interior Design: Sharon Page

All Scripture quotations not otherwise designated are from the *New American Standard Bible*® (NASB®), © copyright The Lockman Foundation 1960, 1962, 1963, 1968, 1971, 1972; 1973, 1975, 1977, 1995.

Permission to quote from the following additional copyrighted version of the Bible is acknowledged with appreciation:

The *New King James Version* (NKJV). Copyright © 1979, 1980, 1982 Thomas Nelson, Inc.

Library of Congress Cataloging-in-Publication Data

McIntosh, Helen B.
    Messages to myself : overcoming a distorted self-image / Helen B. McIntosh.
      p. cm.
    Includes bibliographical references.
    ISBN 978-0-8341-2456-1 (pbk.)
    1. Christian women—Religious life. 2. Self-talk—Religious aspects—Christianity. 3. Self-perception in women—Religious aspects. 4. Depression, Mental—Religious aspects—Christianity. 5. Emotions—Religious aspects—Christianity. I. Title.
    BV4527.M395 2009
    248.8'62—dc22

                                            2009014384

10 9 8 7 6 5 4 3 2 1

CONTENTS

Acknowledgments   7

Introduction   11

1. What Are You Thinking?   19

2. The Self-talk of a Warrior Princess   31

3. Where Did That Come From?   53

4. God's Perspective of the Truth About You   75

5. Helping Your Children Learn Healthy Self-talk   93

6. Peaceful Relationships   103

7. Putting It into Practice   141

Bibliography   157

ACKNOWLEDGMENTS

To the girls—

My sincere thanks to "the girls" with whom I have been sharing these thoughts for several years. Your deep encouragement and love have ministered to me greatly.

To my family—

My earnest thanks to my dear husband, children, and grandchildren for their love and patience as I have taken time and study to become more whole in my heart and mind. It is my hope that as a result of asking God to help me internalize these principles, our family relationships will be healthy and strong. I also thank my precious daughter, Blythe, for her editing skills as well as her encouragement for so long. My deepest thanks go to both of my children, Bryan and Blythe, for helping me grow as they were growing; to my mother, whose wounds helped me to seek healing; and to my dad, a valiant warrior who died as I was writing this material.

To my God—

Thank you, Lord, for your path of deliverance from the lies that affected my thinking and from past and present wounds that resided in my heart. Thank you, too, for your teachings about reconciling relationships. Thank you, Lord, for your clear scriptural models of reframing that you have been whispering to my heart for decades.

Though the fig tree should not blossom
And there be no fruit on the vines,
Though the yield of the olive should fail,
And the fields produce no food,
Though the flock should be cut off from the fold
And there be no cattle in the stalls,
Yet I will exult in the LORD,
I will rejoice in the God of my salvation.

—Habakkuk 3:17-19

The following material is not intended as a substitute for professional counseling but as a help, guide, and encouragement to take a fresh look at your internal "scripts" or messages, and your language with others.

This information offers help for improved personal emotional health and techniques for better communication with others.

INTRODUCTION

Do you feel depressed in some area of your life? Maybe several areas? Are you or someone close to you earnestly afraid or anxious about the real or possible threat of job loss, a health concern, or another type of crisis? Do you feel you have taken on the pain of a friend who is despondent? Do you know someone who has recently given birth and is in the depths of despair? Do you share the pain of someone who has not given birth and desperately wants to? Is it difficult for you to watch the news because you feel depressed about what you see or hear that reminds you of your own situation? Or does it connect with another change or loss in your life—or even another set of issues in your wounded heart? Have you had a hard time getting past the deeply wounding messages from someone you love or have loved? Do you know someone who wrestles with suicidal thoughts? Do you wonder if you matter to God?

Many of us struggle daily in the hidden places of our hearts and minds. The dark and painful thoughts may come from the past, the present, or worry for the future. Some very old wounds may still hurt you as deeply as ever.

One thing is for sure—these difficulties of the heart and mind can cripple us personally in countless ways and can also keep us from having better relationships with one another. You want things to change because you want to escape this pain; but change is uncomfortable and scary. You may even feel that you lack the energy that trying something new in your life will require.

This book is for women who struggle with these kinds of personal issues, such as a poor self-image, depression, anxiety, anger, and even suicidal thoughts. According to a posting on WebMD.com on February 28, 2009, one in ten Americans experience depression. Undoubtedly, there are men, women, boys, and girls who are not diagnosed and are untreated. Perhaps you are a friend or family member of a depressed person, and your life is profoundly affected as a result of that person's ongoing problems. In my case, my mother's life-long anxiety issues have had a lasting effect on me.

The information you hold in your hand can teach you a simple method of viewing your internal "scripts," or messages, in a unique way that will give you the tools for great and lasting changes that will enhance your feeling of mental wellness. What you think and believe directly affects your behaviors, choices, and mental health. You will be looking at the messages in your head and in your heart and will expose any lies lurking there. Even one lie produces damage or destruction.

The desire of my heart is to be a language coach who helps you look at the way you currently speak to yourself and then change any messages that are not true. For example, if you tell yourself that you can never move beyond an emotional wound that was caused by a parent or friend and that you will carry that sadness with you always, the truth is that it is your choice to remain enslaved by those thoughts and your current condition. You have the power to move forward with your life. Yes, you experienced a deep wound, but the truth is that there are a lot of things you can do and people who can help you move through this season and receive a measure of healing. It may take some time, but change is possible. We will examine ways to move in a new direction toward fulfillment and healing.

Many professionals and many books are available that can provide solid information to help you improve relationships. What is often missing, however, is practical and specific language to apply to your own life and to your interaction with others that will increase the health of each relationship. In the second half of this book, you will find many language devices and helpful words to assist you in securing better communication with the difficult persons in your life.

I will also share basic principles of behavior to guide you in work relationships that can be troubled. For example, you are responsible only for kindly and firmly sharing truthful information with others. Their response is about their hearts, not yours. You are responsible for the message you give; they are responsible for the message they send back to you.

You'll learn many new ideas for conversations with persons you find difficult. I will share my "sandwich" mental outline you can follow when sharing a difficult message or stating a correction or objection with friends, coworkers, or family members. My Peace Rug process teaches a language you can employ and can teach young children, teens, or adults to help them find their voices with those who treat them disrespectfully in any way. You'll learn key words to use that will enable you to stand firm in difficult situations.

I'm glad you have chosen to invest in this book that asks you to address the question point-blank, *What am I thinking?*

It is not uncommon to avoid sharing innermost thoughts because of the fear of what others might think about what you think. In this book I will guide you into asking yourself tough questions that you may have been avoiding. I will ask you to consider what it is that causes you to think in making make sense of it.

I'm grateful you've joined me on this journey. I want to tell you why it's so important to look at your thoughts and understand where they can lead you.

You have undoubtedly witnessed the progression of depression in either your own life or the lives of others. Depression often begins with an unresolved issue—perhaps a present or past emotional wound compounded by other sad events or disappointments. Often "people problems" are somewhere in the mix. Are you suffering from hurts that stem from broken relationships, unresolved conflicts, unsettling events, or harsh messages—either spoken or implied?

It's human nature to try to minimize the messages received over time that cause sadness or anger, but after a while the pain becomes cumulative and creates one big, fuzzy haze of darkness in the soul. This can result in eating too much or having no appetite; insomnia or too much sleep; a low energy level followed by fatigue. It can cause low self-esteem and poor concentration. It can cause difficulty making decisions and feelings of hopelessness. It can cause feelings of insignificance and isolation.

Unless you, either alone or with a skilled counselor, deal with the growing haze of darkness in your soul, there will be a growing intensity, frequency, and duration of the symptoms I've just described. It's not okay to ignore even one of these red-flag symptoms. There is so much you can do if you sense even one of these problems in your "internal scripts" or thinking. Ignoring it will not make it go away.

This book will help you become alert to the onset and stages of depression, fear, anxiety, post-traumatic stress, anger, poor self-image, and even suicidal thoughts and will help you take a step—or several steps—to be free of it.

A National Institute of Mental Health (NIMH) study found that half of adults in the United States have a mental or physical condition that prevents them from working or conducting their usual roles for several days each year, and a large portion of those days can be attributed to mental disorders. The study, published in the October 2007 issue of the *Archives of General Psychiatry,* is based on a nationwide survey of 9,282 American 18 or older. NIMH further states that an estimated 26.2 percent of Americans 18 years of age or older—about one in four adults—suffer from a diagnosable mental disorder during any given year.

According to statistics on the WebMD site, depression in women is very common. Those statistics show that women are twice as likely to develop clinical depression as men, and as many as one in every four women is likely to experience an episode of major depression at some point in life. Nearly two-thirds of those women do not get the help they need. It is an epidemic that must be addressed and reversed in order to ensure good mental health for future generations.

I will be sharing with you a method that can help free you from the thoughts and feelings you long to change. What I'm going to share will give you hope and provide true changes for a lifetime.

Following are two more examples of ways the information in this book can work for you.

Loss: If you feel despondent because of a recent loss, maybe the death of a loved one or the loss of your job, you may feel that you will never be okay again. You may feel that life is just too hard and that no one cares about you or what you're going through.

You will learn ways to line up your internal scripts according to truths rather than these lies. One truth I share is that God longs to bring His light into the dark places of your heart and free you from persons or circumstances that control your love, joy, and peace. He wants to free you with His truth regarding what is happening in your heart. Using my Truth Chart, you will gain insights into your thinking and how your thinking affects your beliefs. You will see for yourself ways in which freedom comes to you when you get serious about achieving it. If you are not a Christian, you can benefit from the Truth Chart, but this book is written primarily for the Christian who wants to achieve a higher level of mental and emotional health.

As you work through the Truth Chart, you will begin to think through deceptions and proactively counteract those deceptions. Although you have suffered loss, you can begin to believe that you will be okay, that, yes, this loss is hard but not so hard that you can't survive it and that there are people who care about you.

There may be other deceptions to face such as feeling that you are worthless, that you have blown it with family and friends and cannot recover, and that there is really no point in trying. When these lies creep into your heart and mind, they must not be allowed to fester there, causing additional pain and frustration.

God may show you that there are losses in your life that you need to acknowledge. He will validate your thinking that your losses are greatly felt at 100 percent. He also wants you to feel His assurance that He longs to give you grace for these hard times and hard places in life.

Fear: Are you fearful that you will lose someone or something dear to you—such as your marriage? What is the truth? Sometimes fear can cause you to react to your spouse rather than respond to him or her. Fear of an anticipated unpleasant outcome often produces controlling actions motivated by trying to protect one's heart. Trying to control someone's behavior can often cause further damage to the relationship— causing the very thing you feared to occur. You will learn to look beneath the fear to see a wider range of what might be causing it. Perhaps the fear is a result of insecurities or false or distorted messages you have believed.

This book will help you begin to see yourself as one who has reached for the right tools, and you can re-pattern your thought life to release you from the things that drain you and keep you from the life of freedom that God wants you—and all of us—to enjoy.

Connecting Thinking and Doing

Most professional counselors believe that what you think affects what you do—your behavior, in other words. If that is true, and I believe that it is, then thinking is extremely important, isn't it? Wouldn't it follow, then, that you and I need to know the reason behind our behaviors?

Most persons, though, focus primarily on behavior, thinking they can just quit behaviors they don't like. "Just quit being depressed." "Just get over it." "Just move on with your life."

The truth is, until we can figure out what is causing the behavior, we are likely to continue repeating the behavior.

Just forcing a smile when you are experiencing emotional pain is called "masking" and is not a healthful behavioral choice. I invite you to look behind the behavior or attitudes. I will encourage you to look deeply into your heart and mind—your internal message center—where you harbor your internal scripts. If you look into your internal message center and examine the messages you find there—the good, the bad, the ugly, and the untrue—and make changes to your thinking processes, behavioral changes will follow.

In the pages ahead you will find very practical ways you can alter your thinking and therefore your behaviors. Since I cannot sit down with you and talk to you personally about your thoughts, I will share my experiences to show you the connection between thoughts and behaviors.

What is there in your life that needs to come to the surface so you can deal with it and move on? What messages or images are you dwelling on that are keeping you from the fullness of life that Christ offers? Let's move ahead.

WHAT ARE YOU THINKING?

$\mathcal{I}$ thought I handled the blows in my life and to my sense of well-being with a learned Southern charm and grace: "Well, okay—if that's what you think" or "If that's what you say, then it must be true." After all, why would anyone intentionally wound me or cause me to question his or her words or actions?

I slowly came to realize, though, that not everyone—including my loved ones—understood the power their words had over me or understood that I allowed their words to dominate my thinking and what I believed about myself. Over time, I came to understand that there were feelings and emotions deep inside that I couldn't account for. I didn't remember how or why they resided in my heart, but I wanted to banish them and the damage they had caused.

I didn't know that my thoughts and my behavior were linked in any way. So when I had a specific thought about a person's actions or a word that was spoken to me, I didn't realize how much it affected the way I lived.

The effects of these words and actions also affected the way I viewed relationships—my relationship with myself and my relationships with others. I knew I needed to reframe ("reframe" is a term I use to mean picturing something in a different light) years of pain and frustration, but I had no role model to follow.

The Truth Chart

The Truth Chart process that I developed was initially developed for my own mental health. I began using it in 1970, but it was many years before I began sharing it with others. Now I have almost daily opportunities to share this method, and I have been surprised and humbled by the results. The participants in the classes I teach and those I counsel in my private practice continue to share that they have had dramatic changes in their thinking patterns and behaviors. These individuals have encouraged me to put these ideas into this book so others can experience what they have discovered regarding depression, emotional anxiety, and personal thought life. They have shared that these ideas are novel, concrete, and practical.

For most of my childhood and into my adulthood, I thought of myself as vanilla—you know, just plain vanilla. No sparkle, no color, nothing memorable. Certainly not jamocha almond fudge or white chocolate strawberry—just vanilla.

Many damaging messages were delivered to me by people who were important to me during the course of my life: "Can't you do anything right?" "You're so weak, so stupid, so clumsy . . ." I had internalized those messages, and they had become a major component in my self-talk and poor self-image. Samples of my internal scripts were "I am a zero." "I never do anything right."

In addition to these damaging conversations with myself, I had never really internalized God's view of me either. These became more than just internal thoughts—they became wounds that affected me deeply. The wounds were far deeper than a skinned knee here and there, although there were many of those. The wounds I'm referring to were name-calling, displays of anger and rage, and actions against me.

Since I invited Christ to come into my life as my Savior and Lord many years ago, I've been totally convinced that God loves me and has a plan for my life. I knew He had forgiven my sins and answered many prayers. I've taught Sunday School and Bible studies since my salvation experience, and I have taught biblical life principles to others and believed them as truth. But when I had feelings of not being special or had feelings of not being of value to God, I didn't really label those thoughts as lies. I taught others about guarding their thoughts, but I never really internalized the application of these principles into my own thought life. It wasn't that I didn't believe I was special to God. But there were wounds— deep internal messages from others—that superseded God's messages to me. Fortunately, that has all changed.

Not too long ago I asked God for the name He had for me. I first heard of this concept at a conference by author John Eldredge a few years ago, but I didn't ask God right then. This idea originated in the passage of Scripture from John 10:3 about how "the sheep hear his voice; and he calls his own sheep *by name* and leads them out" (NKJV, emphasis added). I knew it was important for me to hear God's name for me; I just wasn't sure I really wanted to know. I was confident it would be something vanilla.

Recently, though, I decided I needed to know. I didn't hear God's audible voice, but clearly and distinctly, after a time of prayer, came the phrase "Warrior Princess." Wow! Nothing vanilla about "Warrior Princess!" God had reframed my thoughts even about who I am.

We make choices like that every day—every moment of every day. What are we to believe when we have certain ongoing thoughts and feelings? Thoughts and feelings may feel very real. But are they true?

The purpose of this book is to help you be attentive to your thoughts and feelings, but you must not get stuck in reflections and past hurts. Instead, look at your thoughts and feelings from the truth of God's perspective. You are not wiping out the real and honest wounds or reflections or even the in-depth processing of these things that come to your heart and mind. They are to be validated; but don't get stuck there.

Wounds in Action

Once you are able to see your wounds and reflections from God's point of view, you can be freed from ongoing despondency, depression, anger, and anxiety. Remember the word I used earlier, "reframing"? Here's a recent personal story to illustrate what reframing is.

It was the week before I was scheduled to speak at a women's retreat. It was a cold, drizzly afternoon. I had just dropped off my granddaughter at her home and was only a few blocks away. I went through a fast-food drive-through and picked up some large containers of soup, which I put on the floor of my car to take to my mother-in-law.

Traffic was thick, as it always is on this busiest street at the busiest time in the afternoon—bumper to bumper. I have no idea how it happened, really, and I offer no excuses. But before I knew it, I was looking down at the soup that was wobbling on the floor—and I reached for it, consequently bumping the car in front of me suddenly. My car had moved forward—apparently my foot slipped—and I was thrust into one of the most embarrassing moments of my life! It was followed by such personal agony—a genuine shame attack. *I am such a disaster. How could I have done that? I will never be trusted ever again to drive my granddaughters.* A lot of people saw it. I felt totally exposed! I had stopped traffic, and I felt as if hundreds of pairs of eyes were watching and calling me stupid.

❊ ❊ ❊

Hear the wound? Do you hear the stories under the wound? You can hear the ownership of responsibility, but mostly you hear the pain. We'll reframe this in just a minute. Back to the scene.

The man in front of me was not happy. In what seemed only a second he walked back to my car and stood beside me. Oh, he was angry! And I even knew him—and his wife, who was with him. But he didn't let that stand in the way! He quickly called the police, which, of course, you are supposed to do. Within five agonizing minutes we were summoned to drive a short distance to a service station on a corner where twice as many people could see us. There wasn't just one police car—there were two. I was overwhelmed with an all-too-familiar sense of inadequacy and failure, by the feeling of being a bad grandmother. How scary to realize that my granddaughter was in the car only moments before! *I'm too bad a driver to be trusted to drive my grandchildren ever again.* These messages then multiplied and began to connect with my mother's damaging accusations from decades before—her avalanche of accusations over the smallest of infractions. That tender place in my heart was hurting so badly.

Picture me: I stood with the police in the cold, wet rain. It was freezing outside, and I had on several jackets; but because I was fresh from a pedicure, I was wearing high-heeled jeweled sandals—and holding my teacup poodle. How silly I must have looked!

For hours and hours Satan whispered additional messages to the ones I was already having, such as "How can you possibly teach the women this weekend?" My agony was profound. It was time to reframe.

Reframing

I went to God and first said, *Lord, I hurt so badly. I feel like such a failure. I feel like such a zero, so "legally blonde." I'm very okay with the traffic ticket and the fine, and I'm fine with replacing the man's bumper. Those things aren't what bother me. I just hate feeling so inadequate.*

Then I started looking at that accident through God's perspective—period. I began to say to Him, *The truth is—it was serious, but everyone is okay. I was careless, but I am not a failure as a person. God, I am so sorry. I hate what it feels like to be distracted. Lord, could you give me grace to bear this hurt—the grace that I enjoy giving to others but have trouble receiving myself? You are enough for this ouch. Thank you that I am adequate in you; thank you that I don't have to be adequate in my own strength anyway. I would love to learn from this, Lord. I ask you to help me be a better driver. When I think of this accident, I choose to think of the ways I have already grown and choose now not to assume false shame. Thank you, Lord. You are enough.*

This book is about the process of reframing thinking, feelings, and past or present wounds, and it's based primarily on the following two Scripture passages. It's also about restoring relationships—through both your self-talk and your other-talk.

> Though we live in the world, we do not wage war as the world does. The weapons we fight with are not the weapons of the world. On the contrary, they have divine power to demolish strongholds. We demolish arguments and every pretension that sets itself up against the

knowledge of God, and we take captive every thought to make it obedient to Christ *(2 Corinthians 10:3-5)*.

If you hold to my teaching, you are really my disciples. Then you will know the truth, and the truth will set you free *(John 8:31-32)*.

A stronghold is like a worn path—but a path that is created by the *enemy* of our lives. Have you ever taken a shortcut across the lawn again and again? Pretty soon you have created a marked path. When you know you should go a different way but you keep returning to that same path, that is a stronghold. When someone has a difficult conversation with you, and the damage of the conversation is not repaired, you will continue to feel that hurt, that wound, for a long time. Then you develop sensitivity to similar wounds by others, and that, too, is a stronghold.

Maybe you tend to often take on false guilt or false responsibility from someone else's words or actions. False guilt and false responsibility are strongholds. If you have a sad thought, then another and another—and they don't receive attention—it becomes a stronghold. Maybe you're plagued by recurring anxious or fearful thoughts that don't get resolved as the wounds deepen. Those, too, become strongholds. You get the idea of how this pattern can deepen and spread to more than just one area of your life. You have not only developed a stronghold but have also established an *agreement* with your enemy.

It is the truth—biblical truth—that does set one free from these strongholds or bondages. Truth is the only thing that can provide freedom from these "strongholds," "arguments," and "every pretension that sets itself up against the knowledge of God."

Before we explore this, let me clarify that I'm not speaking of truth that some might interpret as positive messages that sound good and cheerful for the moment. Examples of these well-meaning but often damaging messages include "Oh, you can do it!" "You can always get another dog," "Time will take care of that," or "Be happy—you have so much." The reality is that when someone is mad, sad, anxious, or fearful, there's more important information to be gained from the expressions of emotions.

We need to look long and hard at what our thoughts and feelings are telling us about our heart. Just being positive and cheerful could serve only to minimize pain, implying that there is a fast "cure" that is not realistic. Positive messages we give ourselves or receive from others will not have a lasting effect. Only Christ can permanently relieve the hurt of deep emotional pain. Though you can be available for friends and loved ones, and others can be available for you, cheerful counsel and unsolicited advice are not the answer. The mind of Christ is required.

Careful study of the Scriptures, learning scriptural principles, and looking to the Holy Spirit for guidance give us the wisdom to see truth from His perspective.

Truth: Where Does It Come From?

I believe that God is the author of truth, wherever it is found. As a counselor in the public school system for 12 years, I could not initiate conversations about God or use biblical scriptures, but I could talk with students about more general principles of "truth."

It's fascinating to see how truth and reasoning are handled by the secular professionals in our society. In the field of psychology, there is renowned research to show the truth and profound importance of disputing irrational thinking as the main antidote to depression and anxiety. I had been reframing my thoughts and feelings for decades before I found this research, but it confirmed the importance of what I had been practicing to deal with my thoughts. The research states that "cognitive behavioral therapy," or the "disputing of irrational beliefs," is superior to pharmacology, which is using medication to aide in someone's pain management, or even a combination of cognitive behavioral therapy and pharmacology. God's perspective is the ultimate reframing, and it stretches beyond just knowing that irrational thinking should be disputed. The study of secular research and how it underscores the truth of what I'm sharing with you is discussed in more depth in a future chapter.

For now, let's explore more fully what reframing of self-talk is and how to develop a mental outline to help when you are continuing the well-worn path of anger, depression, fear, or anxiety. Conquering these results of self-lies is possible.

MAKING IT PERSONAL

1. A suggested prayer: *Lord, would you open wide my under-standing of the issues of my own heart? Would you help me put a name on my hurts? Would you help me to see the damage? Would you give me the grace to cover this tender time of reflection and exploration of my thoughts and feelings? In Christ's name I pray. Amen.*

2. Don't rush this next step. Take your time. Think about what might be past and present wounds. You can list people, events, circumstances, conversations, anything in your life that has brought hurt.

Past wounds

_____

_____

_____

_____

_____

_____

_____

Present wounds

_____

_____

_____

_____

_____

_____

_____

3. Are there some common themes? What might they be
   called? Some examples: abandonment, rejection, feelings
   of inadequacy. These are possible strongholds.

   _____

   _____

   _____

   _____

   _____

   _____

   _____

THE SELF-TALK OF A WARRIOR PRINCESS

We examined what you and I think about—our self-talk—and how we deal with it, or maybe how we don't deal with it. Let's take a look at where those thoughts originate.

Self-talk is what you say to yourself second by second, whether or not you realize the content of the message. What are the messages you're feeding yourself about you? Are your messages words that come from your Heavenly Father, or are they words that come after you realize you've gained 10 pounds? Are they messages of a warrior princess or the words that reside in deep wounds? Do your messages to yourself reflect truths about yourself, or are they words that others have spoken to you in anger and you have internalized? Scrutinize what you tell yourself; search out messages you've given yourself that make you feel like an orphan—messages that make you feel like someone without a Heavenly Father.

If you don't dispute faulty thinking in your self-talk, you're camping on the subtle path to depression, fear, anger, anxiety, and a host of other emotions you don't want.

For example, if you originate the message "I'll never be able to . . ." you may then internalize a message that goes like this: "I'm such a failure in so many ways."

In the first chapter of Romans we learn of a people in a sad state of affairs. The key to their downward spiral is found in Romans 1:25: "They exchanged the truth of God for a lie."

Further, the Bible tells us that those who "became futile in their speculations" (Romans 1:21), also had depraved minds (v. 28), were full of deceit (v. 29), and were without understanding (v. 31). There are many other effects of exchanging God's truth for a lie, but these verses show the toll on a person's mental health, from God's point of view.

Monitoring Self-talk

The first of two important goals of monitoring self-talk is to recognize faulty or irrational thinking. The word "meta-cognition" means thinking about our thinking, and that's what I'm suggesting. It's very healthy to listen to what's going on in our heads.

Here's an example to help you better understand what faulty or irrational thinking is: A person may say to himself or herself, "I can't drive any farther down the road. I feel as if I'm going to wreck this car." Many persons experience this sort of anxiety—called a panic attack. In fact, panic disorder is fairly common in American adults between the ages of 18 and 54. In the example of the person driving the car, the thing that makes the thought irrational is that unless something is mechanically wrong with the car, the only problem is in the driver's thinking. Anyone can have an irrational thought; wellness exists in knowing how to dispute the thought, abolish it, and change it.

The second goal of monitoring self-talk is to be able to reframe faulty or irrational thoughts so that we can stand in intercession on our own behalf and better understand what God has to say about us. A heavenly point of view gives us a completely different frame of reference.

It's not enough to know that what we're thinking and feeling is slightly irrational. We must not settle for just acknowledging cloudy thinking when there's so much more for us to experience! We must reframe those faulty or irrational thoughts.

When you know what Scripture says about you from God's point of view and know that it's true, you'll be set free.

This important reframing step allows you to begin living as you are meant to live. It's like someone handing you the keys to a dream home that's full of promise, hope, and a new way of life.

In this chapter is the outline of the Truth Chart. It's a powerful and practical tool to help you reframe your thoughts. I suggest you put it into practice on a daily basis.

The chart contains two columns. The column on the left is headed "Thinking." The column on the right is headed "Truth."

You'll notice where you organize your thoughts and record what you're thinking and feeling in the left column. That column is a kind of vertical journal of messages to yourself, where you'll list your most heart-wrenching fears, your deep discouragements, and your losses, both large and small. This is where you'll list and consider the disappointments you've had over time, your feelings of anger, both hidden and apparent, and feelings of general anxiety. The left column is an exercise in being open with God and sharing with Him honestly about the condition of your heart—but without any shaming or blaming. This is not the time for you to be hard on yourself and think *I shouldn't feel this way.*

It's important to be honest before God; while living in this world you and I will have dark, depressed, or flawed thoughts. Record them openly. Try to see this exercise as an inventory of what's going on in your heart.

After you've made this vertical list and spilled out in the left-hand column what you know to be happening in your heart and head, go line by line and write down in the right-hand column what you know to be true. Make an entry in the right-hand column for ever entry on the left. You may be wondering how to do that.

First, ask God to help you see each left-hand column entry from His point of view. You may need to spend more time on some of what you've listed in this column, and some items may require more prayer than others as you dig deeper into God's Word and reclaim the truth. Everything you know about God's Word will become alive. Even if you don't have much knowledge of what the Bible says, you can ask God to show you what He wants you to see in this quest for truth. He will make himself known to you and will reveal himself to you if you seek Him.

One way to practice the presence of God is to imagine a split screen in your head, as if you were viewing a sports event on television. That split screen contains (1) your awareness of God and (2) His perspective. The truth is that He's really always with us if we're believers. Another visual to help you is that of an IPOD docking station or charging cradle that plugs into the dashboard of your car. In order to hear music after you've inserted the docking station or cradle, you must turn the dial to an "unoccupied" station, push a button or two, and you'll hear music. Are you a docking station, awaiting God's message? Following are a number of verses of Scripture that will give you assurance that God longs for you to hear Him.

Verses of Assurance

Isaiah 30:18-21—Therefore the LORD longs to be gracious to you, and therefore He waits on high to have compassion on you. For the LORD is a God of justice; How blessed are those who long for Him. O people in Zion, inhabitant in Jerusalem, you will weep no longer. He will surely be gracious to you at the sound of your cry; when He hears it, He will answer you. Although the LORD has given you the bread of privation [adversity] and water of oppression, He, your Teacher will no longer hide Himself, but your eyes will behold your Teacher. Your ears will hear a word behind you, "This is the way, walk in it," whenever you turn to the right or to the left.

Genesis 3:9-10—Then the LORD God called to the man, and said to him, "Where are you?" He said, "I heard the sound of You in the garden."

Exodus 19:9—The LORD said to Moses, "Behold, I will come to you in a thick cloud, so that the people may hear when I speak with you and may also believe in you forever."

Exodus 20:19—They said to Moses, "Speak to us yourself and we will listen, but let not God speak to us, or we will die."

Deuteronomy 4:30, 36—When you are in distress and all these things have come upon you, in the latter days you will return to the LORD your God and listen to His voice. . . . Out of the heavens He let you hear His voice to discipline you; and on earth He let you see His great fire, and you heard His words from the midst of the fire.

Deuteronomy 5:27—Go near and hear all that the LORD our God says; then speak to us all that the LORD our God speaks to you, and we will hear and do it.

Job 15:8-9—Do you hear the secret counsel of God, And limit wisdom to yourself? What do you know that we do not know?

Job 42:1-4—Then Job answered the Lord and said, "I know that You can do all things, And that no purpose of Yours can be thwarted. 'Who is this that hides counsel without knowledge?' Therefore I have declared that which I did not understand, things too wonderful for me, which I did not know. Hear, now, and I will speak; I will ask You, and You instruct me."

Psalm 32:8—I will instruct you and teach you in the way which you should go; I will counsel you with My eye upon you.

Psalm 63:6-8—When I remember You on my bed, I meditate on You in the night watches. For You have been my help, and in the shadow of Your wings I sing for joy. My soul clings to You.

Psalm 81:13—Oh that My people would listen to Me!

Psalm 95:6-8—Come, let us worship and bow down, Let us kneel before the Lord our Maker. For He is our God, And we are the people of His pasture and the sheep of His hand. Today, if you would hear His voice, do not harden your hearts, as at Meribah, As in the day of Massah in the wilderness.

Psalm 135:17—They have ears, but they do not hear.

Psalm 143:8—Let me hear Your lovingkindness in the morning; For I trust in You; Teach me the way in which I should walk; For to You I lift up my soul.

Isaiah 50:4-5—He awakens Me morning by morning, He awakens My ear to listen as a disciple. The LORD God has opened My ear.

Ecclesiastes 5:1-2—Guard your steps as you go to the house of God and draw near to listen rather than to offer the sacrifice of fools; for they do not know they are doing evil. Do not be hasty in word or impulsive in thought to bring up a matter in the presence of God. For God is in the heaven and you are on the earth; therefore let your words be few.

Matthew 10:26-27—There is nothing concealed that will not be revealed, or hidden that will not be known. What I tell you in the darkness, speak in the light; and what you hear whispered in your ear, proclaim upon the housetops.

Matthew 11:15—He who has ears to hear, let him hear.

Mark 4: 22-24—Nothing is hidden, except to be revealed; nor has anything been secret, but that it would come to light. "If any man has ears to hear, let him hear." And He was saying to them, "Take care what you listen to. By your standard of measure it will be measured to you; and more will be given you besides."

Mark 7:16—If anyone has ears to hear, let him hear.

Luke 14:35—He who has ears to hear, let him hear.

John 10:4—When he puts forth all his own, he goes ahead of them, and the sheep follow him because they know his voice.

1 Corinthians 2:9-16—Just as it is written, "Things which eye has not seen and ear has not heard, and which have not entered the heart of man, all that God has prepared for those who love Him." For to us God revealed them through the Spirit; for the Spirit searches all things, even the depths of God. For who among men knows the thoughts of a man except the spirit of the man which is in him? Even so, the thoughts of God no one knows except the Spirit of God. Now we have received, not the spirit of the world, but the Spirit who is from God so that we may know the things freely given to us by God, which things we also speak, not in words taught by human wisdom, but in those taught by the Spirit, combining spiritual thoughts with spiritual words. But a natural man does not accept the things of the Spirit of God, for they are foolishness to him, and he cannot understand them, because they are spiritually appraised. But he who is spiritual appraises all things, yet he himself is appraised by no man. For who has known the mind of the Lord, that he will instruct Him? But we have the mind of Christ.

Hebrews 3:15—Today if you hear His voice, do not harden your hearts.

Revelation 3:20—Behold, I stand at the door and knock; if anyone hears My voice and opens the door, I will come in to him, and will dine with him and he with Me.

As these verses fill your spirit with statements that show you truth, write the statements in the right-hand column opposite the things you've listed in the "Thinking" column. It's important that every time you're bombarded with thoughts or feelings from the left-hand column, you say out loud, "The truth is . . ." and absorb one of the truths from that right-hand column. That is where you must stand. That is where you must stay. You and I do not have the luxury of staying in the left-hand column. Even though you can look at the thoughts and feelings on the list on the left and recognize that thought as an irrational thought, the clarity of knowing it is irrational isn't enough to bring the ultimate peace and rest you long for. Peace and rest will come when you see things from God's perspective. Then—and only then—truth liberates you.

In the next chapter is a Truth Chart with examples of this mental outline. After a time, you won't need to write down your mental journey unless you just want to. It will soon become second nature to you as you take these steps.

The Truth Chart sounds simple—and it is. We weren't meant to jump through hoops to get clarity in our lives. An important thing to remember is that it's not how well you say it or how nice and neat your chart looks. No one is going to see it but you and God. If you have difficulty claiming the truth and overcoming your self-incriminating thoughts, you may need to spend some time asking yourself why. It might help you to journal some of the reasons that it's difficult for you to put your thoughts on paper. Then ask God to show you truths to help you overcome your hesitancies.

The Truth Chart
Reframing Self-talk That Leads to
Depression, Fear, Anger, and Anxiety

THINKING 2 Corinthians 10:3-5	TRUTH John 8:31-32
I feel . . .	But the truth is . . .

As you begin your own Truth Chart, remember that Christ came for you to live in the truth that's beyond your comprehension. Begin now!

You'll notice as you become familiar with the Truth Chart that if you're spending most of your time in the left-hand column, you're not going to be as healthy emotionally as you could be. If you spend too much time dwelling on the left-hand column, you'll have a tendency to remain melancholy and feel depressed, fearful, angry, and anxious. To shake those feelings, you must do the work to reframe your self-talk.

There's an expression in counseling or therapy: "She's doing the work!" It takes time to do the work, but it's a valuable process to work through our thoughts and feelings. Some people have called it personal inventory, and that's exactly what this is. It's doing the work of lassoing your thinking, writing it down, and taking a look at your self-talk to pinpoint the areas where you need God's perspective.

If you're concerned about someone finding your journal, keep it in a very private place. I'm very visual, and if I don't actually write things down, I'm not sure that I walked through the discipline of collecting my thoughts. Also, if I don't record my journey, then I don't see my progress. I have to see where I've come from, and that's what God wants us to notice. When I write it down, I have something tangible to remind me that I've confessed it to God. You, too, may find it empowering to see it on paper so you can apply that truth language to your life for the next hour, day, or week.

Recording Your Own Truth Chart

I suggest that you keep an ongoing journal in your planning calendar, handbag, or briefcase, and when you realize that you're feeling overwhelmed about something, write those things down in the left-hand column. You might record that you're feeling profound sadness, sheer fright, or lingering anger. Write down exactly what you're feeling and what you're thinking. You'll be amazed at what taking those thoughts captive will do to help you.

Guard against telling yourself that you shouldn't be feeling this way and therefore fail to write it down. If you thought it, "it" deserves some attention. Don't let what you should have done short-circuit your examination of the deeper messages of your heart.

Telling yourself not to think about things that convict or bother you puts a quick covering on something that needs attention. If you did that on a surface wound, you would soon have an infection. Be as open and honest as you can be. That's what confession really is:

Lord, I'm so angry.

Lord, I'm so scared.

Write it down. It's your confession and your honesty before God. No coverings.

Did you ever stop to think that you don't have total control over what you think about? You'll come to see that there are a number of influences that play into your thinking.

One frustration you may have is that you don't want to think about all that you're thinking about! The great accuser—Satan—puts thoughts into your head and seeks to destroy you by gaining a stronghold on your thinking. You must combat his assaults that hold you captive when you believe it's your own weakness that causes you to think about things you don't want entering your mind. You'll need God's help to stand against an enemy who wants you to remain defeated in your thinking.

After recording your thoughts in the left-hand column of the Truth Chart, you will be able to move to the right column. You'll notice that you naturally want to get to the good stuff, and the "Truth" column is a source of freedom, because it gives you another option to the way you're feeling. Take the journey carefully, and involve God in it.

An example of how you might pray for God's perspective as you move from the left to right column is *God, show me this from your perspective, and deliver me from my way of thinking. Another way to ask is Lord, I want to rise above this and look at this from your perspective. Give me your words and your wisdom for this. Flood me with your truth. Show me if there's anything blocking my ability to see and hear from you.*

Ask God to reveal to you the source of darkness that surrounds you and causes you to feel anxious about your thoughts or to dwell on something that's a distraction. When the enemy is allowed to create havoc in our thought life, we miss hearing from God.

You may have heard the comparison of life to a tapestry. If you look at all of the seams underneath the tapestry, it seems like an absolute mess. But then, when you look at the topside of it, it's an organized and beautiful picture. God wants to make a beautiful tapestry of the lives of men and women who conquer their speculations and every lofty thing that raises itself up against the knowledge of God. Those speculations are the mess underneath. God's perspective is the topside of the tapestry. Sometimes we can't see the picture God is weaving—or we feel there's something blocking our vision—because we've failed to grasp the beauty God sees in us. Until you're able to see the "big picture," you can rest assured that His grace is enough, that God's heart is good toward you, and that He longs to bring restoration and recovery.

Warfare

"Be of sober spirit, be on the alert. Your adversary, the devil, prowls around like a roaring lion, seeking someone to devour" (1 Peter 5:8). If he can keep you angry or anxious or scared or unclear about your life, you're not going to be a princess warrior. You'll wear out, which is exactly what he wants you to do. I believe with all my heart that you'll begin to receive blessings and clarity in your life if you change your self-talk. If not, you could get bogged down, focusing only on your thoughts and feelings and not moving forward to the place where you can see yourself from God's perspective. The result could be costly to your friendships, your family, and other deep relationships. Failure to see yourself from God's perspective and accurately assess who He is and His heart for you can also affect your relationship with Him. The enemy is quick to use our wrong thinking to defeat us.

Learn to be alert to your own self-talk. That will take a little time, but it's worth it to take that time and effort to develop awareness of your self-talk. You'll also need to give attention to the process. For example, it's important to take time to go through the process of working through the stages of grief. There are no quick fixes or shortcuts through that process.

As you learn to see yourself as God sees you and change your self-talk, it's not prudent to move so quickly that you miss working through many of your thoughts and feelings. If you don't deal with each step, it would be like medicating only part of it, then sewing it up. It can become infected and cause an even worse problem.

You may have been told, "Oh, don't think about that," "You shouldn't feel that way," "Push that away," or "You really should have moved beyond that by now." If you give in to that way of thinking, you won't process the messages of your heart. It's very important to listen to every thought. You may even see that a pattern has developed, and recognizing that pattern will make it much easier to pick up on your unhealthy self-talk.

Once many of our family members were attending a cheerleading exhibition at a local high school. Hundreds of children were participating in performing routines they had learned during a week of cheerleading camp. We had gone to watch my seven-year-old granddaughter, Sarah, perform her routine. Afterward, as I was visiting with her and sharing in the excitement, I asked her if I could take her to lunch before I went back to work. She declined and told me that she wanted to go back to her other grandmother's instead. My heart was absolutely broken.

I knew in my head that I should not feel resentful or jealous that Sarah wanted to go home and be with her other grandmother (whom I also love), but I'm human. My feelings were hurt. God gave me the grace to be able to say, "Sarah, it's okay to tell me no." I knew in my head that was the right thing to say, and it came almost automatically. But as I drove away,

I was so sad and scared. I was thinking, *Sarah and her parents and little sister are moving here soon. Is this how it's going to be? Is she never going to want to be with me? Does she not love me?* These kinds of thoughts were washing over me, filling me with bad feelings, so I made the deliberate decision to change my self-talk: *Well, this is coming from my weak places, my wounds, my feelings of rejection, and my feelings of not being okay. But the truth is that God wants me to be okay, and He loves me completely. Lord, I rest in you!*

I started praying, *Okay, God—I know that you want me to have victory here. I don't know how you're going to do it, but I'm already resting in the right-hand column of truth, because I know you want me to be okay. You don't want my heart to be anxious.* I was thankful for my own mental outline, stored in my head from repeated use, that I could process while I was driving. I don't always have pen and paper handy.

Because the feeling of rejection is a tender place for me, my mental outline would probably say in the left column, *I feel rejected.* The truth was, though, that Sarah's response was not personal. It *felt* personal, but it was not. If I don't listen to my self-talk and then reframe it, I'm going to be a mess for the years of grandmothering that are ahead of me. I don't want to be angry and sad when what God really wants me to do is extend grace. I knew I needed to get past these kinds of feelings. God allowed me have that little moment (well, it was a pretty big moment) to get my heart prepared for the future.

Here is how God orchestrated more healing after I had moved to the second column from my hurt with Sarah. Soon after this event, I was talking to her on the telephone. We have a tradition of making up a story and tying it to something that just happened. For example, "Once upon a time there was a little girl who was about to move." Or if she had gone to a ballet recital, I might say, "There was a little girl who was wearing a pink tutu." Then we would tell parts of the story back and forth until we brought the story to a close.

So during this conversation with Sarah, I said, "Sarah, do you want to do a story tonight?" She said she didn't want to, and I felt hurt again. As a counselor and as her grandmother, I knew I should applaud her ability to refuse me and to set boundaries if that was how she felt on that particular evening.

I did a quick mental outline and chose—instead of being hurt—to say, "That's okay, Sarah. You can tell me no."

She was very sweet about it, and I said, "We can do it another time. You know Sweetie, it really is okay to tell Nannie no when you don't feel like doing something I suggest."

Then I said, "Are you still concerned that you told me you didn't want to go to lunch that day?" She said she was, and I said, "I wanted to talk to you about that again, because I want you to know I'm okay when you tell me no."

I don't want Sarah to carry false guilt, and I don't want to be a controlling person. What I want is to be a safe person for her. If I start saying, "You can't tell me no," or "That hurts Nannie's feelings," she may begin to hide her feelings because she doesn't want to risk hurting me. That's not healthy for either one of us.

I'm happy to report that now, a few years later, Sarah and I have enjoyed many special times together. We've developed our own unique relationship, as have her sister, Ann, and I.

This is possible only because I made a conscious choice to live in the second, right-hand column.

Honest dialogue happens when the parties know how to properly process hurt. Later in this book we'll look more closely at dialogues and the reconciliation with others that takes place when you've been successful in reframing your self-talk.

Boundaries: Here Are Yours. Where Are Mine?

Reframing your thoughts and feelings will also help you establish healthier boundaries with others. It's common for a person to use the following as an excuse not to set boundaries: "You know, I feel responsible for [a person]." It could be a genuine responsibility that you must meet. However, if you feel overwhelmed, chances are that you're assuming a false responsibility for that person. The truth is that you're not responsible for that person nor that person's love, joy, or peace.

The danger in taking on false responsibility for any situation is that you're keeping the other person from assuming his or her own true responsibility. This puts you on the road to becoming a rescuer, an enabler, and a codependent person. Believe me—it's not a road you want to follow.

God has really had to teach me in this area. Because I'm a Christian, I want to help others. But I'm often not really helping another person if it's not something I'm called to do—even if it makes me feel better or seems like the right thing to do. For example, it's a good thing to extend care—but it's not okay to be a "caretaker." A caretaker is someone who's working harder in the relationship than the person being cared for is working, and the caretaker is rescuing or enabling that person and interrupting his or her handling of responsibility that's clearly his or hers to assume.

If a pattern of your life is to feel responsible for others, you'll benefit from taking a look at what's going on in your own head and heart. Ask yourself, *Is this a need of mine to feel important? Is this how I feel important? Is this how I feel that I matter—to be responsible for this, this, and that?*

Often you'll begin to resent the very person you're trying to help and may get to the point that you don't even want to have a relationship with him or her. After you've reframed your thinking and know you need to set a limit, you could say, "I feel that you're wanting me to take responsibility for [whatever it is], but I can't." You may even want to add, "I can't do this, but I can support you in other ways."

Once you're able to do this, you'll not only feel a huge sense of relief, but you'll also begin to experience relationships that are healthy—the way God intended them to be. You're not responsible for another adult person—that's up to God. When you get in the way of His work, it puts you in places you don't need to be and adds more burdens to your life than you were meant to carry—burdens you probably don't really want to carry anyway. If you're going to walk with a renewed heart and mind, you must look closely at the things keeping you from moving forward. Remember—you may not *feel* like a warrior princess, but that's what you are. Get used to living in that truth.

MAKING IT PERSONAL

1. A suggested prayer: *Lord, will you help me to hear my self-talk today? What am I thinking? What am I feeling? Will you help me start a truth chart? Will you help me not to short-circuit my list by having thoughts that I shouldn't feel this way? I want to have an accurate inventory of my heart and mind. Thank you, Lord. In your Son's name I pray. Amen.*

2. I feel [fearful, angry, discouraged, anxious, grieved, and so on].

_____

_____

_____

_____

_____

_____

_____

_____

_____

_____

_____

_____

_____

_____

3. Take this list before your Heavenly Father, and ask Him to meet with you so that you might hear from Him. The Assurance Verses you read are your confidence that He wants to speak to you about the things you've just listed. He longs to bring you His truth about the things you've written down. Record every insight He gives you.

_____

_____

_____

_____

_____

_____

_____

_____

_____

_____

_____

_____

_____

_____

_____

_____

_____

WHERE DID THAT COME FROM?

Be strong in the Lord and in the strength of His might. Put on the full armor of God, that you may be able to stand firm against the schemes of the devil. For our struggle is not against flesh and blood, but against the rulers, against the powers, against the world forces of this darkness, against the spiritual forces of wickedness in the heavenly places.

Therefore, take up the full armor of God that *you may be able to resist in the evil day,* and having done everything to *stand firm.* Stand firm therefore, having girded your loins *with truth,* and having put on the breastplate of righteousness, and having shod your feet with the preparation of the gospel of peace; in addition to all, taking up the shield of *faith* with which you will be able to extinguish all the flaming arrows of the evil one. And take the helmet of salvation, and the sword of the Spirit, which is the *word of God.* With all prayer and petition pray at all times in the Spirit, and with this in view, *be on the alert with all perseverance* and petition for all the saints *(Ephesians 6:10-18, emphasis added).*

In this chapter I'll address having spiritual victory over your thoughts, your past and present wounds, and your conversations with others and with yourself. You'll learn ways to have victory in battle against the lies of the evil one. You've learned the importance of the truth that leads to freedom so that you can enjoy good mental health. It's worth noting that the first piece of armor mentioned in Ephesians 6 is the belt of truth! You will notice also that truth is linked with standing firm, which is stated three times in these scriptures for emphasis. Stand firm so that you cannot be shaken.

If you stand firm, you have a better chance of being able to recognize what is truth and what is not truth in your life. The peace that comes with truth is a direct result of reframing and reconciliation. And truth is aggressive! If you look more closely in Ephesians 6 at the armor of the soldier described there, you'll see that the sword of the Spirit is "out front." That's the Word of God—again, the truth. John 1:14

offers more on the relationship between the Word and truth. It states, "The Word became flesh, and dwelt among us, and we saw His glory, glory as of the only begotten from the Father, full of grace and truth." Another reference to Word and truth as being one in the same comes from John 17—Jesus' priestly prayer. In verses 15-17 He said, "I do not ask You to take them out of the world, but to keep them from the evil one. They are not of the world, even as I am not of the world. Sanctify them in the truth; Your word is truth."

Truth does set us apart and preserves us from lies. The Ephesians 6 passage closes with "be on the alert with all perseverance." I believe using the Truth Chart can help us do that. If we continually line up our thoughts and persevere to compare those thoughts with the truth, we'll be alert to lies from the evil one.

Attacks That Come Through Wounds and Hurtful Messages

Satan attacks us with lies and also through our past and present wounds. I've shared with you about some of my wounds. Let me ask you this: have you acknowledged your wounds? Have you been able to write them in the Truth Chart and express your feelings about them and what has caused them? Wounds of the heart leave you vulnerable to your own self-pity. Even worse, they leave you ripe for Satan's attacks. Painful events and experiences in your past need to be taken to the second column, or you'll most likely lose the war. If you don't do the work, you won't be victorious.

We can actually create some of our wounds ourselves by making wrong choices, or wounds may be due to family, friends, or difficult circumstances. Either way, they need to be looked at, prayed over, and taken to God for His truth about each one. When I talk with clients about their wounds, some of the questions I ask them are "Do you think you've ever wounded someone and you're still experiencing pain over that?" "Are you repeating some behaviors that either cause you pain or cause pain to others?" "Can we look at what's true about these situations and move toward freedom once and for all?"

Some examples of wounds might be rigid, unloving, or controlling parents; divorce; addiction; abuse by a parent or spouse, whether verbal, emotional, or physical; neglect; profound grief and loss in the death of loved ones; chronic illness; rape during your childhood or as an adult; not finding a life partner; favoritism by a parent toward a sibling; not being able to have children; infidelity; and even financial losses. *These wounds should be recorded in the left column.*

Make the vertical journal or list of these events, thoughts, or feelings. They're important. They're real. They're worth examining. As you proceed, I will show you how then to move to the right column by saying, "But the truth is . . ." as you carefully process each of these wounds.

When depressive thoughts begin, we often don't feel like taking action. We often feel too despondent to think about what to do. This is the time to reframe these thoughts and feelings, which will significantly relieve the depression. Metacognition, or "thinking about your thinking," as discussed earlier, is definitely a proactive step for your mental health; but the key is moving to the second column. If you don't believe what is *true,* then you'll believe a *lie.* If you're living in lies, you're losing the war.

Satan is the father of lies. He's also the author of doubt and discouragement—all of which are located in the mind. His agenda is stated in John 10:10—"to steal, kill, and destroy." There's no battleground more sly than the mind. Satan is also called an angel of light, so we know that an attack is not going to look like an attack. You can count on a deceptive and subtle attack.

I knew I needed to reframe my thoughts and feelings in a major way when my daughter, Blythe, left Nashville for Colorado. She was about to marry the man of her dreams and begin a wonderful new life that God had truly orchestrated. Her father and I were thrilled about her new life too. The wedding was going to be in six weeks from the time she left.

However, out of nowhere I began crying and couldn't seem to stop for days. I was a wreck—way outside the normal range of emotions! I began asking myself, "Whoa—where is this coming from?" Was it about her wedding, or was it about her living so far away? God began to show me that it was the latter.

For more than 10 years, Blythe had lived only a couple of hours away from home, and in my head I had tricked myself into thinking I had done all the letting-go that parents of adult children are supposed to do. However, after some intentional lining-up of my thoughts and feelings, God let me know that I had not *really* let go.

What a blind spot! How thankful I was for the red flag. God is faithful to show us our issues when we're out of our comfort zones—times when we're sad or even in times of celebration, such the example I gave of my emotions in the midst of celebration. We're responsible to say, *God, what is this?* I don't know much Spanish, but one of my favorite Spanish expressions is "¿Qué pasa?" which means "What's happening?"

We're responsible to God for guarding our hearts and for noticing those red flags. In obedience to Proverbs 4:23—"Watch over your heart with all diligence, for from it flows the spring of life"—I began to reframe my thoughts in a prayer. My prayer went something like this: *Lord, I'm despondent—full of grief and sadness in my thinking and feelings concerning my loss of Blythe and the changes ahead. But the truth is—I trust you for this passage. I really do want to believe you for this, and the truth is—I am in a struggle. Please help me let go. Help me do the right thing. Help me see things from your perspective, Lord, as I walk in you today. Show me your perspective. Let me see the top side of the needlework. I don't have to see the whole picture. But I cry out, Lord, for you to give me clarity and give me victory, because the truth is—I know that you want me to be victorious. You don't want me to stay in this condition. It's an appropriate response to loss and change, but you want me to have victory and freedom from this place of bondage.*

Satan works more freely in my life when I'm discouraged and full of doubt, disappointment, and depression—all the D's; that's an earmark of Satan. The evil one does not want me to be effective, but God longs for me to have victory.

So the work I had to do with my thoughts concerning Blythe was *Lord, I don't want to hold her in my hands. I do trust you with her. The truth is that this marriage is what we have prayed for—for many years—so how silly this is!*

Is it not classic how we sabotage ourselves with the assistance of the evil one? When I could finally see this from God's perspective, I could not believe that I was having a meltdown because of an answer to prayer! So I said to the Lord, *Lord, the truth is, I've prayed for this. This man loves her, prays over her, and is going to be good to her. She wants this, so the truth is that I just have to let go of her. I can call her, I can fly often to see her, and I can do some creative things to keep in contact with her.*

It's a mental game. Contrasting lies with truth is a purposeful and deliberate method we can use in cooperation with God to trick the evil one. It's a way of saying, "Satan, you have no place in my life. You have no domain here." I'm not always as instantaneously victorious as I wish, but I'm going to continue choosing to stand with God. I'm going to fight this mental battle in this way. I'm going to choose *not* to hide my dark thoughts.

When you ask God to name or put words to your dark thoughts, He might show you five, six, or even ten thoughts that have contributed to your depression or anxiety. It may not be just one, even though it started with just one false thought that was not lined up with God's truth. We let one thought or feeling just slip in, and before you know it, another one slips in, then another one; and by not taking them over to the second column, they become a tangled mess. The truth is—we know where to go, and we know the answers lie with God. *But we need a system or method of seeing our thinking from His perspective.* We need a concrete way to step out of the *lies* and live in the *truth.*

This is what the Truth Chart is all about. Up until now, you've had thoughts on both sides, but you probably haven't known where those thoughts should land. I felt the same way, which is why I developed a method for keeping track of these thoughts. Many people will tell you, "Oh, cheer up," or "You don't have anything to worry about." But the reality is that we *do* have thoughts that need to be looked at—not quickly brushed aside and ignored.

Sometimes we stuff our thoughts and feelings because we don't know what to do with them. We're unskilled in thinking inside our own heads. Sometimes we let our thoughts and feelings stack up because we're in a hurried lifestyle, and we don't take the time for this kind of personal inventory. Sometimes we stuff our thoughts and feelings because we lack a "safe" person to talk to about our dark thoughts. However, when our thinking stays hidden from ourselves and others who could possibly help, it's a dangerous place to be, both mentally and spiritually. It puts us on the dark side.

Where Does Our Thinking Come From?

Where do the thoughts in the left column come from? First, they're messages that someone has given to you either directly or by implication. Unhealthy people in your life—including your family members and friends—hurt you by giving you these messages in what they've said or done. Second, you have given certain messages to yourself as a result of misreading messages that others have said to you that were not intended to hurt you. Sometimes we're our own worst enemy, because we make these deductions and cause many wounds to ourselves.

Third, these anxious, depressing, or "dark" thoughts are a result of living in a negative world. We're bombarded daily with subtle and not-so-subtle messages from advertisers and other media that communicate that we're not okay unless we use their products. Another twist of negative messages is the assault of violence in programming today, including news media. Fourth, we receive these messages from the evil one.

For example, I had a lot of negative messages from my mother. Many were implied messages, although she actually said many times that I was a zero and that I could not do anything right. When you hear messages like this from important persons in your life, from the world, from the enemy—you may begin to think and feel things that lead to your own sense of failure.

That's not looking at your messages from God's perspective. You must go to the second column. For me, this would look like *God, you know I feel like a failure today, but the truth is that I know that I'm not a failure. I may have made some mistakes, but I'm not a failure. You call me a work of your grace. You call me Princess. You call me Warrior. You've permitted this brokenness in my life, but you don't want my failures to discourage me. You long for me to be victorious over this, and you'll give me the grace to bear it.* In other words, you just put down as many things as you know are true as an antidote.

Another example in the left column is "I feel so rejected . . ." Then you move quickly to the second column and say, *But the truth is that even though this feels like rejection, it's not rejection. Something about me has touched a place in them that they did not know how to handle. It was their inability to handle this, and it touched a place in them that's not okay.*

These are examples of taking a thought and replacing it with truth. If, however, this is not done, the build-up of thoughts and emotions is like a dam that backs up and causes the truth not to flow as freely as it should. It could lead to further problems that eventually cause a malfunction. The same is true for us.

Thoughts and Behaviors That Can Destroy Us

Suicidal thoughts and eating disorders are battlefields in spiritual warfare. Neil Anderson and Timothy Warner's book *The Beginner's Guide to Spiritual Warfare* says it this way:

> Jesus made it clear that Satan came to steal, kill, and destroy, so it is not surprising that Satan would suggest to people he attacks that they kill themselves. Suicide is a growing problem in the world. A surprising number of teenagers confess that they have had more than passing thoughts of taking their own lives. It is the third leading cause of death among young people aged fifteen to twenty-four. It is the eighth leading cause of death among people of all ages in our country (91).

One of the most widespread diseases for women that affects two out of three women today is eating disorders—whether overeating, anorexia, or bulimia. In their lifetime, an estimated 0.5 percent to 3.7 percent of females suffer from anorexia, and an estimated 1.1 percent to 4.2 percent suffer from bulimia. Surveys conducted by the National Institute of Mental Health have estimated that between 2 percent and 5 percent of Americans experience binge-eating disorders in a six-month period. This is a common stronghold in the lives of women, because it's a battle of the mind over the image a woman has over herself. It's clearly a spiritual battle.

God has made us in His image, and believing anything less about yourself leaves you open to the lies of the evil one. Overeating is a subliminal need to comfort yourself and to fill up the empty places in your heart and life. Overeating is a counterfeit substitute for the wholeness only God can give. It is a legitimate need, but the need is falsely filled.

The only way to combat these lies is to speak truth against them. If you don't journal your thinking in the left column and then go to the right column with the truth, you'll continue the cycle. Never dealing with the pain and attempting to anesthetize it are not "cures"—they're idolatry, choosing something in place of God. You're looking to other people, places, things, events, and circumstances instead of receiving love, joy, and peace from God.

Our culture is obsessed with thin people. Add to this the need to be loved and accepted, and you have a perfect setup for anorexia. A woman feels as if she's not important or successful unless she's thin—but that's a lie. We see images of emaciated women on magazine covers who are searching for significance in all the wrong places. No matter how thin they become, nothing is enough to give them a lasting sense of significance, and they continue in a downward spiral until they have to be hospitalized. A recent study by The National Association of Anorexia Nervosa and Associated Disorders shows the mortality rate among people with anorexia has been estimated at approximately 5.6 percent per decade, which is about 12 times higher than the annual death rate due to all causes of death among females ages 15-24 in the general population.

There's enormous peer pressure to be thin. In order to be accepted by peers and not considered or even referred to as fat, many young women go to extreme measures to control their weight. Anorexia is a disease about control. For some, eating or not eating is one of the few things in their lives they feel they can control. An example would be a young person who is having a difficult time in school or with people in her life over whom she has no control. She can control what she eats, however. If a child has an overly controlling parent, he or she may rebel by choosing not to eat. In the child's mind, this rebellion is justified because the parents control every other aspect of his or her life. Every person needs to feel some measure of control for his or her own life. But taking control to extremes—whether you're controlling someone else or you're the one who needs to reestablish control in your own life—can destroy relationships and wreak havoc in vulnerable hearts.

Are you seeking to control your children beyond what's healthful for them or for you? When you're not feeling your best—perhaps depressed or anxious—do you press into your children with more control? Children are keenly aware when parents go overboard controlling the kids as a substitute for having control of their own lives.

Another control issue related to anorexia that's even subtler and produces an even deeper stronghold shows up in the person who has developed anorexia and begins a thought pattern fueled by the enemy: *I don't deserve to live. If I eat, then I'll live. Therefore, I won't eat.* These thoughts come straight from the evil one.

When we feel out of control about any number of things and fail to take those thoughts to God, we try to "take control." Instead of saying, *Lord, I'm in a mess,* or *Help me, God—order my life; order my steps,* we start trying to control other people in our lives or to control events. There's a lot we can't control, and there's a lot we're not supposed to control.

We know we should not try to control *people,* but, we reason, we *can* control our food intake. It becomes a power control issue. Many find they want to extend their control into one area because they fear losing control in another area—or have already lost it.

Coercion and control in relationships take many forms, all of which cause damage. One of the more subtle forms is that of hidden expectations—either expectations we have of others or expectations that others have of us. I'll go into that more in a future chapter. The basic idea is that when we entertain any expectation of how someone else should be toward us, that person will feel it as control. Moreover, if that person doesn't perform as we expect, we'll feel some level of anger. A healthy principle—a way to guard your heart—is to be alert to holding any expectations of others and choose not to go there.

The Battle for Your Life

Spiritual warfare is really a battle for your life. If you continually give in to Satan, there's surely danger ahead. He'll lure you into his own traps more and more deeply, which can result in buying into the thinking of a dark world known as the occult. I've talked to individuals who have gotten into the occult and have found the way out, and many of them have said they began their journey into the occult with heavy drug use. Because these drugs are mind-altering, a door to the spirit world opens and gives way to demonic activity.

The Bible teaches that we live in a spiritual world. It's all around us. Spirit beings are in and around you, your home, your workplace, your loved ones, and your world. The desire of the evil one is to "steal, kill, and destroy" and I believe is often the source of stirring up wrong desires for drugs and then leads the person to destroy himself or herself. The Scriptures say that "Your enemy the devil prowls around like a roaring lion looking for someone to devour." The passage then goes on to say, "Resist him" (1 Peter 5:8-9). We must be alert to the devil's schemes and not fall prey to them.

Cast all your anxiety upon Him, because He cares for you. Be of sober spirit, be on the alert. Your adversary, the devil, prowls around like a roaring lion, seeking someone to devour. But resist him, firm in your faith, knowing that the same experiences of suffering are being accomplished by your brethren who are in the world *(1 Peter 5:7-9).*

The beginning of this dangerous journey is when a person gets to a place in life where he or she feels there's just no way out, the anxiety is too great, the pain is too great, the peer pressure too strong, and life is too hard. That person may begin to mask or apply a Band-aid to the pain by using addictive drugs, and that opens the door to the spirit world. Then messages come into the person's way of thinking, and the messages are not from God—they're satanic, and they say, "You don't deserve to live."

I suggest that we do a lot of deliverance praying for ourselves, our children, and our families. I've prayed the following prayer or something similar for a long time: *Lord, in the name, power, authority, and shed blood of your Son, my Savior, Jesus Christ, I pray that you would rebuke and bind Satan from working in my life in any way, and in the lives of my children, my friends, and other loved ones* [pray for them by name]. *I pray for a divine hedge of protection around them.*

In his book *Waking the Dead,* author John Eldredge offers a daily warfare prayer that he prays for his family and his staff that's one of the most complete spiritual battle prayers I have seen:

My dear Lord Jesus, I come to you now to be restored in you—to renew my place in you, my allegiance to you, and to receive from you all the grace and mercy I so desperately need this day. I honor you as my sovereign Lord, and I surrender every aspect of my life totally and completely to you. I give my body as a living sacrifice; I give you my heart, soul, mind, and strength; and I give you my spirit as well.

I cover myself with your blood—my spirit, my soul, and my body. And I ask your Holy Spirit to restore my union with you, seal me in you, and guide me in this time of prayer. In all that I now pray, I include [names]. Acting as their head and intercessor, I bring them under my authority and covering, and I come under your authority and covering. Holy Spirit, apply to them all that I now pray on their behalf.

Dear God, holy and victorious Trinity, you alone are worthy of all my worship, my heart's devotion, all my praise and all my trust and all the glory of my life. I worship you, bow to you, and give myself over to you in my heart's search for life. You alone are life, and you have become my life. I renounce all other gods, all idols, and I give you the place in my heart and in my life that you truly deserve. I confess here and now that it is all about you, God, and not about me. You are the hero of this story, and I belong to you. Forgive me, God, for my every sin. Search me and know me and reveal to me any aspect of my life that is not pleasing to you, expose any agreements I have made, and grant to me the grace of a deep and true repentance.

Heavenly Father, thank you for loving me and choosing me before you made the world. You are my true Father—my creator, my redeemer, my sustainer, and the true end of all things, including my life. I love you; I trust you; I worship you. Thank you for proving your love for me by sending your only Son, Jesus, to be my substitute and representative. I receive Him and all His life and all His work, which you ordained for me. Thank you for including me in Christ, for forgiving me my sins, for granting me His righteousness, for making me complete in Him. Thank you for making me alive with Christ, raising me with Him, seating me with Him at your right hand, granting me His authority and anointing me with your Holy Spirit. I receive it all with thanks and give it total claim to my life.

Jesus, thank you for coming for me, for ransoming me with your own life. I honor you as my Lord; I love you, worship you, trust you. I sincerely receive you as redemption, and I receive all the work and triumph of your crucifixion, whereby I am cleansed from all my sin through your shed blood, my old nature is removed, my heart is circumcised unto God, and every claim being made against me is disarmed. I take my place in your cross and death, whereby I have died with you to sin and to my flesh, to the world, and to the evil one. I am crucified with Christ, and I have crucified my flesh with all its passions and desires. I take up my cross and crucify my flesh with all its pride, unbelief, and idolatry. I put off the old man. I now bring the cross of Christ between me and all people, all spirits, all things. Holy Spirit, apply to me [my wife and/or children] the fullness of the work of the crucifixion of Jesus Christ for me. I receive it with thanks and give it total claim to my life.

Jesus, I sincerely receive you as my new life, my holiness and sanctification, and I receive all the work and triumph of your resurrection, whereby I have been raised with you to a new life, to walk in newness of life, dead to sin and alive to God. I am crucified with Christ, and it is no longer I who live but Christ who lives in me. I now take my place in your resurrection, whereby I have been made alive with you, I reign in life through you. I now put on the new man in all holiness and humility, in all righteousness and purity and truth. Christ is now my life, the one who strengthens me. Holy Spirit, apply to methe fullness of the resurrection of Jesus Christ for me. I receive it with thanks and give it total claim to my life.

Jesus, I also sincerely receive you as my authority and rule, my everlasting victory over Satan and his kingdom, and I receive all the work and triumph of your ascension, whereby Satan has been judged and cast down, his rulers and authorities disarmed, all authority in heaven and on earth given to you, Jesus, and I have been given fullness in you, the head over all. I take my place in your ascension, whereby I have been raised with you to the right hand of the Father and established with you in all authority. I bring your authority and your kingdom rule over my life, my family, my household, and my domain.

And now I bring the fullness of your work—your cross, resurrection, and ascension—against Satan, against his kingdom, and against all his emissaries and all their work warring against me and my domain. Greater is He who is in me than he who is in the world. Christ has given me authority to overcome all the power of the evil one, and I claim that authority now over and against every enemy, and I banish them in the name of Jesus Christ. Holy Spirit, apply to me the fullness of the work of the ascension of Jesus Christ for me. I receive it with thanks and give it total claim to my life.

Holy Spirit, I sincerely receive you as my counselor, my comforter, my strength, and my guide. Thank you for sealing me in Christ. I honor you as my Lord, and I ask you to lead me into all truth, to anoint me for all of my life and walk and calling, and to lead me deeper into Jesus today. I fully open my life to you in every dimension and aspect—my body, my soul, and my spirit—choosing to be filled with you, to walk in step with you in all things. Apply to me, blessed Holy Spirit, all of the work and all of the gifts in Pentecost. Fill me afresh, blessed Holy Spirit. I receive you with thanks and give you total claim to my life.

Heavenly Father, thank you for granting to me every spiritual blessing in the heavenlies in Christ Jesus.

I receive those blessings into my life today, and I ask the Holy Spirit to bring all those blessings into my life this day. Thank you for the blood of Jesus. Wash me once more with His blood from every sin and stain and evil device. I put on your armor—the belt of truth, the breastplate of righteousness, the shoes of the readiness of the gospel of peace, the helmet of salvation. I take up the shield of faith and the sword of the Spirit, the Word of God, and I wield these weapons against the evil one in the power of God. I choose to pray at all times in the Spirit, to be strong in you, Lord, and in your might.

Father, thank you for your angels. I summon them in the authority of Jesus Christ and release them to war for me and my household. May they guard me at all times this day. Thank you for those who pray for me; I confess I need their prayers, and I ask you to send forth your Spirit and rouse them, unite them, raising up the full canopy of prayer and intercession for me. I call forth the kingdom of the Lord Jesus

Christ this day throughout my home, my family, my life, and my domain. I pray all of this in the name of Jesus Christ, with all glory and honor and thanks to Him (223-26). <www. ransomedheart.com> Used by permission.

It's prayers like this that fend off Satan and put him in his place—far from us. I encourage you to begin praying a similar prayer for your life and for the lives of your family members today.

We must regularly sharpen our discernment concerning the messages we give ourselves that likely come from the enemy. He is the one dividing your home. He is the one leading you into depressive thoughts. He is the one nudging you to leave your spouse. He is the one whispering to you that you don't deserve to live and shouldn't eat, that you should avoid God and others, and encourages the most extreme form of punishment—suicide.

It's serious business when these lies overtake us in such a sly way. The truth is that when we feel our loved ones are in battle, it's our mission to be intercessors. When God brings it to your attention that you should pray against evil warfare—do it. Become a warrior for your own heart and for your family!

Remember earlier when I told you about God giving me the name "Warrior Princess"? There's so much to uncover when God calls your name.

When I was a young girl, I wanted to be a frontier woman or cowgirl so badly. My cousins lived outside Dallas on a farm, and every summer my brother and I would crawl around on large boulders with our cap guns playing cowboys and Indians with our cousins. How I treasured those times of adventure! It's said that the memories you have as a child tell who you really are. I wish I had held onto that mental picture and let my heart remember how much I loved those "warrior" days. At some point, as I grew up I forgot adventure and became a "vanilla" personality.

When God told me that I was "Warrior" and "Warrior Princess," I was amused and flabbergasted. It was then that God reminded me of the little girl with the cap gun and even the adult who invented the "Peace Rug" for victims of bullying. I'm vanilla after all—a warrior! The Peace Rug is described in more detail in a future chapter, and I'll discuss its use and effect as we move through the book. God gave it to me to use with students and clients and victims of disrespecting as a tool to help them find their own voices and take loving but firm stands against such assaults. God's name for me was a complete, total opposite of the view I had of myself of being plain vanilla. My mind was operating where the subtle war was being fought—and the vanilla message was a lie from the pit of hell.

The deception *felt* real. I spent decades being a people-pleaser, caring too much what others thought, and erasing me. Since I became a Christian, God has helped me find some grit and fire to override my codependent tendencies and poor boundaries. Over the years I've reframed those weak areas of my life, and that has been such a gift to me and to my family. I learned and grew in ways I never would have dreamed of as I weeded out the lies that were at the root of my previous choices and behaviors. The truth is—I am a warrior! You are, too, if you belong to Him.

As we move ahead in the next chapter, I'll give you some more visual examples from the Truth Chart so you can begin to recognize parallels with what's going on in your life and begin to practice techniques that will help you begin to do the important work of reframing.

MAKING IT PERSONAL

1. A suggested prayer: *Dear Lord, would you reveal to me now some new levels of truth in my heart and mind? Would you show me the issues of my life that are outside the normal range? Would you show me ways to wage the battle for my own life? Would you show me things and behaviors in my life that I'm minimizing? Would you reveal to me darkness in my heart and mind? I'm going to be very still and quiet and allow you to speak to my heart.* _____

_____

_____

_____

_____

_____

_____

_____

_____

_____

_____

_____

_____

_____

_____

_____

_____

_____

2. Rewrite and make personal the warfare prayer in this chapter. _____

_____

_____

_____

_____

_____

_____

_____

_____

_____

_____

_____

_____

_____

_____

_____

_____

_____

_____

_____

_____

_____

_____

GOD'S PERSPECTIVE OF THE TRUTH ABOUT YOU

We have looked at what affects your thought life, how to combat lies with truth, and the significance of recording your thoughts in the Truth Chart. In this chapter I'll share specific examples from clients who have given me permission to share with you what has helped them get through the tough situations and thoughts in their life. My hope is that this will help you with your own Truth Chart and that you'll begin to see these things on your own for the real truth that's to come.

In my work as a counselor, friend, and mother, I've had opportunities to share the Truth Chart with those with whom I come in contact. Over the years, I've kept a mental journal of how some of my self-talk and the self-talk of others have moved us into knowing actual truth from believing the lies we started with. I want to share some examples with you in hopes that it will be helpful to you as you begin your own journey of looking at emotions, circumstances, and events in your life from God's perspective.

THINKING	TRUTH
I feel so scared about my future.	But the truth is that the future is uncertain for everyone. I can pray and trust God for this. I can ask someone for help in thinking through some of my choices.
I miss my child who lives far away.	The truth is that it is sad: this is both a great loss and a huge change. However, I can call, write, and think of creative ways to build the relationship that I might not do if she lived near.
I feel like a failure.	The truth is that I have made some mistakes, but I am not a failure. I can ask God to help me to learn from my mistakes. God is my adequacy anyway.

I'm remembering hurtful messages from my past.	The truth is that these did cause great pain, but I can choose not to repeat the damage by giving others the same hurtful messages. I can also take each one of the messages and reframe it with what is true about it and what is not true. Then I can ask God to give me the grace to put these messages behind me and in time forgive those who hurt me. The evil one wants me to focus on these painful memories instead of on God and His grace.
I feel so alone.	But the truth is that I am not. God is waiting to meet the needs of my heart. There are other people I can reach out to when I feel like this.
I feel so hurt by _____.	The truth is that he or she did hurt me, but I don't have to stay in this condition. I can ask God for help. In a respectful but firm way, I can tell my offender(s) that they have hurt me. I can read, take a walk, rest, or take care of myself in other ways. I can invite someone to do something fun. I can be okay.

I feel anxious when I walk into a room full of people.

The truth is it is overwhelming, but I can have one conversation at a time. I can go from one "safe" person to another at a pace that is comfortable for me. If I feel uncomfortable, I can leave the room. I also need to breathe well and try to relax.

There are times when I feel anxious while driving.

But the truth is I can drive another mile; then I can stop and get something to drink or eat and walk around until I feel okay again. I can also remember that when the anxious thoughts come, I can change the "channels" in my head and think about something else. God does not want me to feel afraid. I can pray.

I feel like a zero, a nobody, of no value.

But the truth is that God says I am a princess, holy and blameless. He made me to glorify himself. There is a design and purpose to my life.

I feel unlovable.

But the truth is that God says I am His beloved.

I feel tired and depressed.	But the truth is I do need rest if I feel tired. It's okay to take care of myself and go ahead and rest. The feeling of depression may or may not be because of the need for rest. If I still feel depressed after I rest, I will take a look at what's going on in my heart and mind.
I feel depressed.	But the truth is that something is going on, and God would want me to have clarity on what I'm feeling. Is it the weather? Am I disappointed in a relationship? Is it my circumstances? I can ask God to show me what the issue (or issues) are, and then I will take each one and ask the Lord what needs to happen to make me feel better.
I feel so guilty [when I know I am really not].	But the truth is that this is called false guilt. I am responsible for _____ but not _____.
I feel like such a failure in this relationship.	But the truth is that I know I have done all you have shown me to do, God. I cannot control the other person—I can control only me.

I feel so responsible for this person in my life.	But the truth is that I need help with my boundaries. Lord, what am I responsible for, and what am I not responsible for with this person?
[Post-Traumatic Stress] I am having recurring nightmares about my husband's accident with his electric saw.	But the truth is that I can thank you, Lord, that I was there at the house and could run to help him. God, you planned for me to be there to help him. The truth is that it was horrible, but I will eventually be okay. Jesus was there beside me and wept too.
I cannot eat. This is more than my wanting to be thin. If I eat, I will live, and I don't deserve to live.	But the truth is that God wants me to live and has a wonderful plan for my life. It is the evil one who wants to destroy me or have me destroy myself. I do deserve to live. God gave me breath.
I am so sad and angry: my family didn't notice all the things I did for them today.	But the truth is that these are signals that I am having expectations of my family. I don't want them to be prisoners of my expectations, just as I don't want to be a prisoner of their expectations. I will continue to do my work "unto the Lord," not expecting praise or thanks. If it comes, that will be extra.

My husband is working late again, and I feel so abandoned.

But the truth is that his working late is about him and not about me. It is his choice to handle his workload in this way. I can lovingly share with him my concern about this, but I can also look at this time as a gift for me to connect with friends or read a good book.

I'm so sad about the way my adult children's lives are turning out. I feel so responsible.

The truth is it is a grief to see my children not make good choices. However, their choices are not my responsibility at this point. I have faithfully shared with them other choices they can make, but I can't make them choose the better way. I can pray for them. This isn't the end of their storie—these are only chapters.

I shouldn't feel this way . . .

But the truth is that I do feel this way. I shouldn't condemn myself for feeling this way. The feeling or thought is a red flag to look deeper and to see what the real issue is. If I shame myself for feeling or thinking this way, I will not find the truth below. I am choosing to go deeper and not short-circuit the feelings and thoughts with a shame message to myself.

I feel so profoundly sad about my miscarriage.

The truth is that it is a deep grief. It is so common, but women scarcely talk about it. My arms feel so empty. I may never know why my baby died. Lord, thank you that you will comfort me during this terrible season of loss and change and broken dreams. Bring me your grace and strength and hope. Restore my heart.

Now I'm pregnant again, but I'm scared. What if I have another miscarriage?

But the truth is that this is a different chapter than before, a different story. Even though I don't know the outcome this time—I choose right now not to fear, not to doubt your love. Lord, I choose complete trust. Please extend supernatural grace as I walk into my doctor's office again. I will not flinch.

I feel shame because of being sexually abused.

But the truth is that it was not my fault. It was not my choice. It is okay to tell what happened. I didn't say no at the time because I was scared, and I didn't get away, but I can speak up now. I am a survivor. I can be whole again. I can tell my story and teach others to speak up. It is false shame I feel, since I was the victim. Lord, will you heal me of the memory?

Scriptural Applications

Now that you've seen examples of self-talk and how it affects your daily life and beliefs, I want to help you apply scriptures to the Truth Chart. I believe this will give you even greater power to stand against the wrong messages to yourself when you need help the most.

Here's how you can reframe Bible passages as you discover meaningful passages that speak to your heart. I'm using verses that may be familiar to you from 2 Corinthians 2. You may need to practice this several times until it becomes your own way to claim God's promises for you in Scripture to use against your own thinking. Hopefully this will become second nature to you and will be a reminder to you that you aren't going through your thoughts and emotions alone. Jesus felt all of what we feel, yet He went to His Father when He needed perspective. A verse many have memorized is Jeremiah 33:3—"Call to Me, and I will answer you, and I will tell you great and mighty things, which you do not know."

Following is the Truth Chart with the two columns in it like the one you just read. Just to refresh your memory, the left column is for your thoughts. The right column begins with the words "But the truth is . . ."

THINKING	TRUTH
(2 Corinthians 4:8) I am afflicted in every way. I am perplexed.	But the truth is— I am not crushed. I am not despairing.
(2 Corinthians 4:9) I am persecuted. I am struck down.	I am not forsaken. I am not destroyed.
(2 Corinthians 2:16-17) I am losing heart because the outer man is decaying. I am having light affliction.	Our inner man is being renewed day by day. It is producing an eternal weight of glory far beyond all comparison.

Are you starting to see some patterns? Once you have your own Truth Chart filled in with the appropriate scriptures that address your thoughts and emotions, you'll want to keep it in a place where you can refer to it often as you add more scriptures along the way. One of the best tools you can invest in is a concordance that allows you to search scriptures based on key words or phrases. For instance, if you're feeling lonely, then you would go to the word "loneliness" and see the Scripture references listed. You'll find that many of the emotions you feel or thoughts that have come to you can be addressed in Scripture.

You should also ask Jesus to show you what He wants to show you when you come to Him and ask questions about what's on your heart and mind. He'll be faithful to reveal it to you. It's important to write out your thoughts, and I encourage you to do so. But it's also crucial that you go to God and ask Him to make you aware of what He wants you to see. He'll often lead you to scriptures that directly relate to how you're feeling. When you journal and pray, don't forget to ask Him for what He wants to give you in Scripture and in His own words.

What Well-known Therapists Agree On

Christian counseling materials often lack literature and information gleaned from secular studies that offer a higher level of validation and insight. If we don't consider these studies and learn from them, then Christian counselors run the risk of being included in the "pop psychologist" category, implying that we're not scientific and not credible. I'll share with you just a small portion of relevant secular material that I believe will bring even more understanding. This material will help you appreciate the Truth Chart as a valuable tool to reframe the messages you give to yourself.

I've studied hundreds of books and articles in the process of earning my doctorate in counseling psychology. I want to show you how the Truth Chart lines up with some of the most renowned therapists on the subject of depression. There's a lot of agreement on the research that points to the use of cognitive therapy as the most effective for depression. Cognitive therapy is therapy that looks at disturbances in the mind coming from faulty cognitions (thoughts) and/or faulty cognitive processing (what you tell yourself about what you're thinking). So it's basically faulty thoughts and faulty self-talk, which we've already said leads to faulty behavior. It's a vicious cycle that must be broken for lasting mental health and wellness.

As for treatment, most cognitive therapists say the remedy is found in various corrective actions. Even though cognitive therapy is used for many problems such as depression, anxiety (panic disorders, social phobias, obsessive-compulsive disorders, and post traumatic stress), eating disorders, and attempted suicide, I'll address depression primarily.

One of the leaders in the field of treatment for depression is Aaron Beck. He recommends cognitive therapy, which centers on your thinking, as I've done. The authors of *Science and Practice of Cognitive Behavior Therapy,* Clark and Fairburn, state that Beck's cognitive therapy for depression was based on the assumption that the affected people engage in faulty information processing and reasoning and subscribe to schema (beliefs) that are self-defeating. In particular, depressed people are subject to what Beck called the "cognitive triad," in which they have feelings of pessimistic helplessness about themselves, the world, and their futures. The aim of the cognitive therapist is to identify and then help patients correct these distorted ideas and also improve their information-processing and reasoning (15).

Beck's primary work with depressed patients has been in the area of their thinking or processing. Beck's model is known as the most successful one regarding depression, and his distinction is that he identified the faulty or distorted information and how the individual structured his or her world. With his clients, he identified what was going on in their minds and taught them to refute their faulty thinking. In addition to recording their thoughts, he encouraged his clients to engage in various homework assignments that helped them recognize how they got off track in their thinking about a situation or circumstance and how that led to their depression.

Other cognitive behaviorist therapists such as William Glasser, a friend and mentor who developed "Reality Therapy," and Albert Ellis, who speaks on "Rational Emotive Behavioral

Therapy," are concerned with "thinking" in their approaches to the treatment of depression. Glasser says that the person who is "depressing" is *choosing* to do so. I agree that if you remain in your left-column thinking, you're choosing to stay in that condition. It's imperative that you move to the second column in the Truth Chart.

Ellis is known for disputing "irrational or faulty information." It's a big step to reconcile yourself to believing that your thinking needs disputing, but I'm suggesting that the Truth Chart is meant to be the next step to take after you see your thinking as faulty or irrational. You can dispute your thinking as being labeled irrational, but until your thinking is reframed by the truth, there's little movement or lasting change in your thinking. If the truth in the second column can be exchanged for your faulty information in this intentional and organized way, dramatic results occur. This additional step that you do on your own is what liberates and truly changes your thinking.

My response to all of this information is essentially that I'm pleased to see how powerful cognitive processing is by acclaimed therapists, whether the therapy is given with or without medication. The scientific evidence is very strong. Even more profound is the effect reframing thoughts has on the likelihood of relapse.

It makes sense that in repairing the cognitive damage, you would go back to the places in the mind where you "jumped track" (left column) and then make the repairs in the right column (truth). Moreover, if secular cognitive behavioral therapy is this powerful, how much more powerful are God's truths in changing our thinking! He is the best disputer of irrational thinking. His truth is the plumb line, the absolute measuring stick of what is rational and what is irrational. How much more will God's truth liberate us from depression!

This is the reason I'm suggesting the use of the Truth Chart to assist you as you process your thinking. My "corrective action" is this Truth Chart. As best I know from my research, it's a unique method to track daily your faulty thinking in the left column—and then goes the extra step of providing you with built-in correction in the right column, using several applications filled with the language of grace. This is unlike other secular or Christian treatments, which usually just focus on your thoughts and emotions without a practical and lasting method of dealing with them appropriately.

You'll hear many say, "Just be happy in the Lord," "Think about something else that's more pleasant and makes you happy," or "Just do more for the Lord, and you'll feel differently." These are pat answers and approaches that tend to focus on someone not being "spiritual" enough, when the truth is that he or she has very real emotional needs that must be uncovered. Some books by counselors even preach to the person reading it and force a course of action that feels punishing, causing the individual to feel even more guilty for his or her emotions and more helpless to do anything about them. The Truth Chart does neither of these but presents a balanced view of the most successful way to reshape your thoughts and emotions according to the truth that comes from God himself— not a counselor's opinion.

The truth of God is not unique to me; and thankfully, it's available to anyone who asks! God gives truth and wisdom liberally to all who ask (James 1:4-5). Therefore, lining up truth and lies has been widely discussed by many pastors, priests, Bible study leaders, authors, and clinicians over the years.

However, the Truth Chart does more than discuss the best way to do this. It actually shows one how to see from a completely different perspective all that comes into the heart and mind. It gives the person the "language" to be able to do this and see from God's perspective rather than his or her own.

Many professionals say to "claim" a verse when the lies come to mind or to think positively. But I've met with many individuals who feel this type of counseling is mechanical and lacks methods to truly help them think through what's at stake in their thought life. Just applying a verse to a situation without looking deeply into the situation often feels like masking a problem with a spiritual fix. Quick fixes don't get to the source of the problem—even if they have a spiritual tag or label on them.

The Truth Chart goes deeper to help give you the words to apply to your situation beyond someone just handing you a Scripture verse to memorize. Of course, Scripture is vitally important, but if you're given a verse and are expecting it to be enough to address the many facets of your thought life, you need to know there's more that God has to say to you than just one verse. He wants you to ask Him to speak personally to you in that consistent, inner voice that we know is from Him. This comes when we spend time with Him and invite His truth into a situation using the approach I'm sharing with you. Truth comes from Scripture, the personal application of the verse, and God's words to you.

At this point you may be saying, "I believe you! Where do I sign up? How do I sign up my children?" That's where we'll go next.

While you're working through your Truth Chart, you may want to share this liberating tool with others, including your children—who may have their own set of thoughts, emotions, and behaviors that are sometimes more than you can handle or want to deal with. You may have prayed for your children for years without seeing tangible results. Let's talk next about how this newfound information applies to your children and can lead to peace of mind for both you and them.

MAKING IT PERSONAL

1. A suggested prayer: *Lord, please train my brain to recognize irrational or faulty thinking. Please increase my alertness to it. I'm also giving you permission to flood my thinking in ways you wish to speak to me to share truth. I long to see and hear truth as never before.*

2. Review the Truth Chart and examples in this chapter, and select several entries of personal interest. Think about asking God to give you deeper insight into entries for the second column—maybe sentences, paragraphs, or even pages. This will be good exercise—training, if you will—to sense God's perspective. Remember: this is a function of the Holy Spirit, and there's no such thing as right or wrong answers. Remember, though, that we're not trying to generate or manipulate truth, but we're asking God to share His frame of reference. _____

   _____

   _____

   _____

   _____

   _____

   _____

   _____

3. Can you think of some examples of irrational thinking that you've heard this week? In each example, what was the truth? Go ahead and go to God with those examples, and record your new perspective. _____

_____

_____

_____

_____

_____

_____

_____

_____

_____

_____

HELPING YOUR CHILDREN LEARN HEALTHY SELF-TALK

If you watch the news even semi-regularly, you're aware that anger is becoming more and more prevalent in teenagers and even very young children. We make jokes about the "terrible twos," but what's being seen often now in very young children can be categorized as depression and anxiety. I've become accustomed to hearing children speak of feeling sad or angry, having repeated nightmares, experiencing fear, and worrying. This is becoming so pervasive that it seems to me the chances of children experiencing these feelings and emotions are high. The good news is that you can help your children learn to reframe these depressive and anxious feelings—just as you're learning to reframe your own.

Severe examples of children who experience advanced depression and anxiety are brought to our awareness from time to time. A nine-year-old girl in Brooklyn, New York, stabbed her eleven-year-old friend to death after they fought over a pink rubber ball. An article in *Newsweek* (June 13, 2005), said this about the killing: "For experts on youth crime, the killing was another instance of what they view as a burgeoning national crisis: the significant rise in violent behavior among girls."

Certainly this young girl had some depressive and anxious thoughts before and after she murdered her friend. But what would lead a child to take such drastic action? Are adults who are in the lives of these youngsters not noticing their anxiety, anger, and depression?

In Tampa, Florida, a seven-year-old child beat his baby sister to death because he was jealous of the attention she was getting. Where is the breakdown in verbal communication that's leading to acts of violence in children?

If not exposed to acceptable choices to deal with emotional issues, children will react in the ways they observe their peers reacting—even violently. The *Newsweek* article previously mentioned went on to say that "schoolyards, where boy bullies once reigned supreme, are increasingly arenas for skirmishes between girls. . . . Research suggests that the best predictor of violent behavior . . . is not hours logged playing videogames or competitive pressure, but firsthand exposure to violent behavior. And social scientists warn that the number of children who see guns, fights, and other kinds of physical abuse on a day-to-day basis is on the rise."

So how do parents nurture and give attention to the needs of children who are living in a world where violence is happening all around them? What is the best way to help children process what they're feeling as they experience depression, anxiety, and other emotions?

Giving Children Tools to Express Themselves in Healthy Ways

First, if children are old enough to read and write, they can learn to do their own Truth Chart. Help them draw or write down their thoughts and feelings in the left column. Just completing this will help them clarify some of their issues and also help you understand what's going on with them. Real improvements come, though, when you can help them move to the second column—again, by either drawing or writing—and guide them to see what's true about their feelings or situations. You'll be amazed at the change in their faces and behaviors. They'll be free, and children radiate this liberty even more than adults do.

If you're helping a child who does not yet read or write or draw, you can explain the process by using the child's hands. As the child shares his or her thoughts and feelings, one at a time, point to his or her left hand. Then as you take the child to what's true about his or her situation, point to his or her right hand. Sometimes, if appropriate, I hold the child's hands and lift his or her left or right hand and address what would ordinarily go in either the left or right column. This visual activity is meant to give children a concrete way of seeing their problems and solutions. It gives them hope and encouragement. The new perspective helps children not to feel stuck in their thoughts or emotions as they begin to do this activity with their hands on their own.

Other word pictures you can give to a child to help him or her understand the process include the following:

- The ability to stop bad thoughts from entering your mind is like opening and closing a door. You choose it. If you're miserable, you're free to change how you feel by moving your thoughts to the right-hand column.

- The ability to stop bad thoughts from entering your mind is like a soldier guarding his or her heart with a shield. Protect it with all your might!

- The ability to stop bad thoughts from entering your mind is like changing channels—and you have the remote control. You have 100 percent of the power to choose where you are in your thoughts.

Praying for Children

Another powerful step for parents, in addition to helping them reframe their thinking, is praying a spiritual warfare prayer over your children who are having nightmares. Help them focus on and stand firm on God's promises, such as "Greater is He who is in you than he who is in the world" (1 John 4:4). It's important to teach your children to reject dark thoughts, particularly in the form of nightmares, through what God says in Scripture about who we are in relation to our enemy. As Neil Anderson and Timothy Warner say in their book *The Beginner's Guide to Spiritual Warfare,*

Demons especially like to use this tactic [appear in thinking] with children. Children are very impressionable and can be frightened rather easily, especially at night. When children report seeing "things" in their rooms, parents often look around and report that there is nothing or no one there. They don't consider the possibility that the child really is seeing something in his or her mind with a spiritual vision that doesn't depend on the physical organs of sight (90).

Mothers have shared with me that they had begun to think of their child's nightmares as routine or normal but now see that it's warfare. These mothers are now praying specific spiritual warfare prayers for freedom!

Earlier we looked at examples for adults to recognize and exchange faulty thinking for freedom and truth. And we've talked about the importance of giving this to your children as well so they'll have the tools to let go of the anxious and depressive thoughts that are holding them captive. If you fly on commercial airlines, you've witnessed the flight attendant standing at the front of the plane and showing you how to use the oxygen mask in case of an emergency. The instructions are always to put your own oxygen mask on first before assisting a child who is seated next to you. This is to ensure that you have equipped yourself in order to be able take care of the child. A child doesn't have the same skills you have to protect himself or herself in case of an emergency. It's the same with equipping them for how to live without fear, anxiety, and unrest.

Here are some examples of the work that children can do with thoughts and feelings:

THINKING (or left hand)	TRUTH (or right hand)
I am so sad because I can't see my dad. He's in jail.	The truth is that it is sad and it's not the way it's supposed to be. He loves me, and he's missing me too. He'll be back. I can draw pictures for him and mail them. I'll be okay.
I'm dreaming that something terrible is going to happen to my mom.	But the truth is that it's from a bad movie. It's fantasy. It's not real. Mom is okay. Mom is safe.
I'm afraid I'll get lost and the bus won't bring me home.	But the truth is I will get home. The bus driver has a walkie-talkie and cell phone and can get help if he or she needs it.
I will get very sick.	But the truth is that I'm not sick. I'm only worrying about being sick. If I ever get sick, Mom will get medicine from the doctor and will take care of me.
I get scared about people fighting in my house.	But the truth is that this has never happened. If it should ever happen, I can tell them how I feel and can ask for them to get some help.
I'm sad that I can't see my dad. It's hard for me to do my schoolwork.	But the truth is that Dad wouldn't want me to be sad at school. Also, it's not helping. It's affecting my grades. I'll see Dad again. Things will be better soon. This is my time to do more reading.

I am angry about bullies on the bus.	But the truth is that I can say, "Stop!" I can say, "When you bully me, I feel disrespected. I'd like you to stop—can you?" I can report it to the bus driver if someone continues to bully me.
I'm afraid of tests.	But the truth is that even though they're scary, I'll just do my best. If I get scared, it will make me do worse on the test. So if I can relax, I'll do better. Worrying about the test makes my score worse. The truth is that I need to relax!
I'm afraid I won't know the material on the tests.	But the truth is that even though I won't know every answer, I can just do my best. I've worked hard, so I'll know lots of the answers.
I have nightmares about scary things.	But the truth is they're not real. I can count, or I can think about fun things, movies, or books I like.
I'm afraid of the dark.	But the truth is that I'm safe. I can ask for a small light to be on, or music or another sound to help my heart to be okay. I can pray and ask God to help me feel safe.

I miss Mom.	But the truth is that I'm not safe with her until she gets better. I can write letters and begin an album of photos. I can let her know how I feel and ask her to get some help.
When I'm alone, I get scared.	But the truth is that I don't have to stay scared. I can pray, read books, and call a friend. If I need help, I can call 911 or a neighbor. I can also tell my family that I'm not ready to stay alone yet.

It's important to review several times with children the discoveries they make in both columns. They may even restate many times what you've uncovered in both columns.

You may think, *Will this really help my child? He's [She's] only five years old. How would he [she] know anything about depression?* I want to say that not only does this work the first time you try it, but it's also a sustained method that has been proven to work on children as young as four years old and on an ongoing basis.

I've used this extensively in my work as a counselor and have seen it change children's thinking many times over. It's not enough to just walk through this once or twice with children. It should become a part of your daily life with one another, especially as your children face all kinds of evil and unpredictable influences in their thoughts at school, at play, and in the many activities with other children. They're exposed to so many different words and actions that developing a language to express their thoughts and praying with them is their "armor" at a young age. These are essential to their mental health.

MAKING IT PERSONAL

1. A suggested prayer: *Lord, would you please help me to have a supernatural alertness to the children in my life and to really hear the issues of their hearts? Would you provide opportunities for me to help them reframe their hurts and anxieties? Thank you, Lord, for preparing me and for preparing them for this exercise.*

2. As God brings you numerous opportunities to help children with their concerns, think about inviting yourself in to their situations as you begin speaking with each one. For example, you could ask the child, "May I help you? I hear a lot of sadness [fear, anger]. I'd like to share a way for you not to hurt so much. I'll explain how it works, and then you can do it yourself whenever you need to." Write down below other things you might want to say to a child in your life. _____

   _____

   _____

   _____

   _____

   _____

3. Practice a couple of reframing examples from the chart that was shown in this chapter. Ask God to give you additional insight for your responses.

4. If you know of some children having nightmares, would you consider asking the parents to pray spiritual warfare prayers over their children? If age-appropriate, children can be taught to pray themselves. You can pray intercessory prayers for them as well.

PEACEFUL RELATIONSHIPS

We have devoted the previous chapters to reframing your thoughts and helping your children reframe theirs. It's time to move now to your "other talk." I believe this is crucial to restoring relationships with others. It's important that you've taken steps to take care of your own heart and mind, and now we'll move to looking at the ways you relate to others so that your relationships can be all you want them to be.

It's important to dig deeper into the fact that we can't have healthy, peaceful relationships with others until we're set free in our own thinking. Only then will we be free from depending on what others think of us or basing our self-talk on what others say about us.

Only after we're living in the second column of truth more than the first column of self-talk are we more equipped to have healthy relationships with others. This also allows us to help others when called upon to be an instrument of healing in their lives based on the truth we've learned. As seen early on in this book, we can sometimes do more damage than good if we offer quick fixes and unsolicited advice to a friend or loved one. The best way to know if your input is welcome is to ask for permission to share your input. I generally ask my clients or friends who are talking with me about a specific situation, "Is it okay for me to share my thoughts?" or "Is it okay if I make a suggestion?" Instead of sounding as if I think I know it all and that they should think I know it all too, asking for permission to share gives the other person the option of refusing my offer.

One of my favorite verses from the Bible about how we're to respect one another and express the heart of Christ to another in our relationships simply says,

Now I exhort you, brethren, by the name of our Lord Jesus Christ, that you all agree and there be no divisions among you *(1 Corinthians 1:10).*

When a relationship has been weakened or broken for whatever reason, we're called to restore the relationship. It may not be fun, and it may not be what we have in mind, but God's will is that we make amends with one another and not have divisions. My desire is to give you some language to help make that happen. We cannot, of course, force others to reconcile with us or not be divisive, but we can control our language, our body language, and our tone of voice.

The following verse also speaks to the fact that we're to look at restoring relationships in the same way that Christ looks to restore us to himself.

> If anyone is in Christ, he is a new creature; the old things passed away; behold, new things have come. Now all these things are from God, who reconciled us to Himself through Christ and gave us the ministry of reconciliation (2 Corinthians 5:17-18).

Scripture says that if we can be reconciled to Him, then we will *have the ministry* of reconciliation. I believe this is what your heart longs for—wherever you are in your relationship with Him and the difficult people in your life. Relationships are very key elements in our lives, and we were created for relationships. Most persons who think of being stranded on an island by themselves, void of all relationships, come back to the realization that they really do want to maintain good relationships in their lives and accept the work of maintaining those relationships.

I suspect you want to be a walking ministry of reconciliation, and it's hard work. It's rarely fun. It does not seem fair at times to be the one in a relationship who is more alert to the problems, but God has gifted you with the tools to do so, because He trusts you to be able to carry through.

Reconciliation

I'm going to give you here some language to equip you for reconciliation. Reconciliation is not only possible—it's also expected. God knows that we need to do this with one another, and He modeled it in Scripture. Read these verses from His Word that call us to use the language of grace:

> If you have been raised up with Christ, keep seeking the things above, where Christ is, seated at the right hand of God. Set your mind on the things above, not on the things that are on earth *(Colossians 3:1-2)*.

> Put them all aside: anger, wrath, malice, slander, and abusive speech from your mouth *(Colossians 3:8)*.

> Put on a heart of compassion, kindness, humility, gentleness and patience *(Colossians 3:12)*.

> Let your speech always be with grace, as though seasoned with salt, so that you will know how you should respond to each person *(Colossians 4:6)*.

The last two verses are critical words for your own mental health and for the health of your relationships. They are critical *choices* you must make daily, hourly, and moment to moment. Let's look at the choices we make and their impact on behavior.

Choice Theory and Reality Therapy

William Glasser has been one of the best resources in my academic life whom I've become acquainted with over the last several years. He is a well-known psychiatrist who pioneered one of today's leading schools of psychology, Reality Therapy, based on his "Choice Theory" principles. I've studied his work in the field of cognitive behavior therapy, which is the study of the effect thinking has on behavior. Two of his best books are *Choice Theory: A New Psychology of Personal Freedom* and *Warning: Psychiatry Can Be Hazardous to Your Mental Health*.

I am Reality Therapy Certified and have made its language part of my counseling work in schools, homes, and churches over the years. The heart of Reality Therapy involves four basic self-evaluation questions and is widely taught to school personnel to use with students, staff, or parents. However, these principles apply to one's home life and personal relationships. I think you'll find them revolutionary as you talk with others and ask these questions of yourself. As I share each one, you'll want to note how important our thoughts are to our choices of behavior.

For example, let's say a boy is choosing not to do his job in the classroom, such as sitting in his seat and listening to the teacher. We'll assume that the teacher and the student have a good relationship—that's an ongoing goal of most teachers and a goal I extend to parents to foster a good relationship with their child's teacher.

The first question the student might be asked by the teacher in a gentle tone of voice is "What are you doing?" The teacher, of course, already knows what the child is doing or not doing, but the teacher asks so the student can assume some responsibility and acknowledge it. If the student won't answer or is having difficulty, the teacher can state it himself or herself, saying, "I see you're choosing to _____" and state what happened or is happening in a few words. Again, the tone of voice and body language must be respectful.

Another question is "What do you want [need]?" This is my favorite question to ask a grumpy student. He or she is expecting a lecture, and instead, I'm asking what he or she wants or needs. You often get very valuable information from the student's answer to this question. If you truly believe that every behavior is for a reason and is someone's best effort to get certain needs met, then this is good information to have. You've gone straight to the heart of the message behind the behavior. I often ask this question first and then ask the *doing* question second. Whichever works best in your particular situation is the better choice.

The third question is "Is what you're doing helping or hurting you to get what you want or need?" After this helpful self-evaluation question, you'll want to give the person some time of reflection. The light bulb will come on, and he or she will realize the sabotage to himself or herself. Most always the individual answers, "It's not helping me."

You then proceed to question four: "What is a plan—or what do you need to do—to make things better?" Notice where you're placing the responsibility for developing a plan to make things better. It's on the person who has not chosen well, whether that's a loved one, friend, or yourself. You're not telling the person what to do. You're not being bossy or controlling. You're also facilitating the person's higher critical thinking skills.

There are times I go straight to this fourth question when I'm in a time crunch. It's a gentle question for loved ones to use with one another. The next time when something's not working for you, you can even ask yourself *What do I need to do to make things better?* It's a powerful question.

The person then uses his or her thinking to choose a different behavior because he or she sees the needs, sees what he or she is doing, and sees what's not helping. These are skillful questions and should be delivered by you without any shame, blame, or criticism in your voice toward others or yourself.

In fact, Glasser has a lot to say in his choice theory books about a management style, called external control, that destroys relationships. Criticism, complaining, blaming, and other negative attempts to control outcomes and people are evidence of external control. Because this is a destroyer of relationships, I want to show you a way to avoid external control with your family members. I believe its effectiveness is felt throughout the family, and you'll be surprised at how much your children will become engaged in what you're doing and discussing.

Weekly Family Meetings

In many schools, "classroom meetings" are conducted by teachers. During my work as a school counselor, I encouraged teachers during many staff development in-service meetings to hold such meetings and taught them how. Soon I began to see the value of adapting that model for use in homes as well.

These weekly meetings are designed to help bring the participants closer in relationship as well as have consensus about many issues in the home, such as rules, chores, and routines. Whether you're the parent or teacher (or both), you'll want to be thought of as a "safe" person. That means the children don't perceive you as bossing, punishing, complaining, coercing, blaming, nagging, or criticizing them.

These elements are developed further in William Glasser's book *Every Student Can Succeed.* His point is that these externally controlling behaviors destroy relationships. The nagging, blaming, and criticizing are basically defeating your children, whether they come from you or someone else. So meeting regularly and connecting with children and adults in a good way helps build your relationships and overrides the negative influences. Additional learning about each other's needs, and then learning the means to get them clarified and expressed, takes place under these conditions in an open meeting.

Don't you love it when your boss, teacher, or someone else in a position of authority calls you in and asks your opinion on how things should operate? It gives you the chance to say what's on your mind and possibly be a part of the solution. That's the same model as these weekly meetings with your children or other adults in your life. These "others" need and want to be able to express how they feel as you listen to them.

One of the first meetings in a school classroom will involve deciding on the rules that the classroom will use throughout the year. Similarly, a home will also have these meetings to determine chores, routines, and common beliefs. However, before the tough business of solving classroom or home issues, you need to have some fun. A great agenda for every meeting is to form a circle and go around and let each person talk about the best thing that happened to him or her all week. The next go-around might be to tell about the hardest thing that happened that week.

Other ideas for connecting conversations could be what food you would like to be, what kind of animal you would like to be, a favorite present you once received, what you want to be 10 years from now, and if you could miraculously do anything in the world, what you would want to do.

Finally the time comes to talk about those necessary rules, agreements, chores, routines, and so forth. I suggest that teachers or parents ask students or children if they would help establish the rules or core beliefs for the year. You can even ask them to pitch their ideas.

The facilitator will say next, "What is it that we want to have happen this year (either in the classroom or in the home)? What is it we do not want to have happen?" Most children tell you immediately, and they even come up with better rules than you would! The best part is that they take ownership, and you don't have to be the heavy.

After the rules are summarized on paper, you can have the children sign it like a contract. Then, for the rest of the year you can loop back into those agreements that were made.

When teachers and parents need to talk more specifically about chores that the children will do, here are some ideas about language to use. Ideally, the first time you would discuss family jobs, it might sound like this: "Here are the jobs we have in our household, but the way we've been doing the family chores is not working out very well. How do you see us dividing up the jobs? Would anybody have any ideas about a better way for this to work?" This would be for older children, of course. Younger children can still take an active part in the rule-making as you wisely facilitate that with wisdom and respect.

With small children you might say, "Who knows what jobs we need to have happen in this house? Who has some ideas about how this should work? How do you see this happening?" You receive their input, and the response is phenomenal. Children of all ages are so creative in this process, because it doesn't feel coercive. You reach consensus before you leave the discussion, just as you would in a business meeting. For example, if someone says, "No, I don't want to do that job," you can say, "Well, which jobs would you be willing to do? This job needs to happen daily, but you can choose when you do it daily if we can agree on a plan. In our next family meeting next week, we can see how everybody feels about his or her job, and we can brainstorm to see how it could be better or easier. Two of you may decide that you want to combine jobs to make it better."

The goal is to invite discussion among the family members. The relationships are more important than the jobs. The relationships are much more important than having things your way if the objectives are met. You will not be known as controlling if you help facilitate the rules or jobs instead of dictating them. Even with toddlers you can say, "Here are the things that Mommy needs to have happen today." "What do you think we need to do first?" "Let's do it together until you learn how."

Giving Feedback

My granddaughter Sarah imitated me years ago. In an effort to never be a know-it-all or a bossy grandmother, I've tried hard not to give my advice right off the bat. After some space of time, I may say, "I've been thinking about what you said, and may I share some of my thoughts?" It's my effort to stall any answers in order not to be a controlling person. In order to help put the brakes on my tongue, I began saying, "Hmm." One day Sarah said, "Nannie, you always say, 'Hmm'!" She noticed!

What we're talking about is a business model with your being a good manager. You've been to meetings with a moderator who lets you talk, and then he or she summarizes and collects the information into some useful form. Many facilitators use sticky notes for the purpose of letting others share ideas, and then these ideas are grouped and summarized. The home model I'm suggesting is for the parent to ask something like what was outlined with the family meetings, even using sticky notes for the children's ideas if age-appropriate. It might sound something like "We need to talk about how this could work better. What ideas do you have? What was wrong with the former plan?" Then listen. This is a wonderful activity to communicate how important the members of your family are and that you do value their input. Don't you want to have the legacy of being a good listener?

Not Ignoring the Elephants

When it comes to communicating the importance of the family members, even with adult children outside the home, you can say, "What I want is a good relationship. Could we talk about this certain thing we keep bumping into? I'd like to share some areas of concern, but what I want is for us to do well in our relationship as we talk about these things, and I believe we can work this out." Even with adult friendships, one could say, "Can we talk? What I want is for us to be at peace with each other. I feel there's an area we need to fine-tune. Could we talk about this?" "How do you see us handling that better, so that you don't feel this way and I don't feel this way?" You actually talk about the discomfort caused by whatever the thing is that exists between you. You talk about the brick walls; you talk about the problem.

Your posture is one of a clarifier who is being brave and bringing up the family secrets. A wonderful book about that subject is *An Elephant in the Living Room*, by Hastings and Typpo. Anything that others won't talk about that's bringing damage to the relationships and the health of the family or friendship needs to be addressed.

The important thing is to do it in a way that invites participation. If you're seen as trying to be "in charge," others may not feel inclined to participate. Sometimes you can pressure others to comply, but is that what you want? Do you want outward compliance from others, while on the inside they're resenting your coercion? Or do you want others to cooperate because they've chosen and desire to comply, all the while preserving the relationship? The latter feels better, doesn't it?

The relationship is so much more a priority than the family rules or even being right. Family rules are important just as rules are important for schools, businesses, and communities to function smoothly. The rules, however, cannot become bigger than the relationships. The creative way is to keep talking and keep fine-tuning when things are not working. Again, you pitch as often as you can, "What I really want is for us to get along well and to have a good relationship. What is it that we need to do to make things better?"

The truth is that once the relationship is better, the rules are easier to negotiate anyway. Resistance is down and cooperation is up. This is what you want, because it builds relationships rather than just enforcing a strict discipline of rules. Adults don't like living continuously under the burden of a bunch of rules. Neither do children. Harmonious living in cooperation is something all parties can respect and is best for building and sustaining good relationships.

Apologies

Over the years, whenever I realized that I had offended or hurt one of my family members, my heart was eager to make amends. I have had to apologize to my family so many times. I can't say that I liked it, because I didn't like knowing I had hurt someone. I remembered what hurt felt like—wounds from friends and family had been embedded in me over time. I also didn't like making mistakes, because I didn't like feeling that I had blown it. Blowing it seemed to prove that my mother was right after all. Her messages to me were that I couldn't do anything right. For a long time I didn't know how to reframe those messages, but I can reframe them now. And so can you.

It was painful to injure my loved ones, but it turned out to be an instrument God used to accomplish much in my own heart as well as in my family. It was after many seasons of apologies on my part—heart-wrenching and earnest apologies—that I realized what was really taking place. I was having the opportunity to model the habit and routine of asking my very small children for forgiveness—constantly! Then I began to notice my children, Bryan and Blythe, apologizing to each other, using my very words. *Thank you, Lord!*

Also, I learned gradually—and I'm still learning—that it's okay to make mistakes. Here are the simple words I said to clear things up: "Bryan and Blythe, Mommy was wrong to hurt you by [name the root problem or offense, not just the surface issue]. I'm so sorry. Will you forgive me?" I learned this from attending a large national conference called The Institute for Basic Youth Conflicts, taught by Bill Gothard. What wonderful language to bring restoration! All three parts are important. If we just say, "I'm sorry," it's not as powerful as saying, "God has shown me that I've been unloving and not respectful, and I'm so sorry."

Other examples of naming the root problem: "I've been prideful about this," "I've been thoughtless," "I've used a sharp tongue lately," or "I've not had a grateful spirit." You don't really have to go into a lot of detail, but naming the basic offense or offenses is a good practice and helps both parties. The offender needs to take ownership of the offense, and the offended one needs to hear the offender "own" the offense. It's a classic win-win situation

The Bumped Cups

A visual picture that God gave me years ago to help me—and to help me to help others—take full responsibility for what was truly my responsibility is a set of two coffee cups bumping against one another. What spills out of each cup after the bumping is what was in that cup. I cannot blame the other cup for what spilled out of mine. I can honestly say someone "bumped my cup," but I must take responsibility for everything that comes out of my cup or heart. Your issues are yours, and my issues are mine. It isn't truthful to say, "You made me mad." It's more truthful to say, "We've bumped on this issue, and I chose to be angry."

Anger is the result of something not happening a certain way or not happening the way we wanted it to happen. Put another way, there's been an expectation of how things should be, but things didn't happen that way. Anger is a very normal response to disappointment, but after the initial feeling or immediate response of anger, each person is responsible for a better choice than anger. God will give grace, but He expects you to take full responsibility for what's in the cup and what came out of the cup. It's important then to reframe what came out of your heart and move quickly to the second column of truth in your mental chart.

Ephesians 4:26 cautions believers not to let the sun go down on anger. You must take care of your heart—your anger—very quickly. Verse 27 cautions that if you don't, it will become a stronghold. It's important to make the choice to reframe all that comes out of your cup.

The Sandwich

One of the neatest mental pictures—or word pictures—that God has given me over the years is what I call the "sandwich." It's a mental outline to deliver a difficult message to someone.

First, you share something positive. That soft message is the top bun. You sprinkle it with all the honest positives that come to mind. Those are your sesame seeds. Then comes the hard part: the difficult message. You couch that message as your "concern." It is the meat of the sandwich. Then move quickly to another bun of positives. I've used the sandwich many times with parents to whom I must deliver a difficult message regarding their child.

It would sound something like this: "Thank you so much for coming to this conference. We all want your son to be successful in school, just as you do. Let me share some of his strengths with you [the top bun]. We do have some concerns about his behavior [the meat], but we think that if we work together, we can help him to be more successful [the bottom bun]."

Here's another example of the sandwich outline that you could use with someone who continues to wound you. You want to talk about the barriers so the relationship has an opportunity to have healing. Again, you can't orchestrate the outcome, because the other person may not choose to become less controlling or less verbally abusive. But you can take the courageous step of initiating honest conversation about the problem.

It could sound something like this: "What I want is a strong [good] relationship. Is that what you want as well? Would you be willing for us to talk about the things that get in the way of us having that relationship?"

Whether you have tough dialogues ahead with small children, teenagers, adult children, or step-children, you will want to remember to put the relationship first. Many parents have reframed the need for dialogue by saying the difficulty *felt* so personal, but the truth is that it was not. "They're not treating me well" is what the left column might read, but the right column is "But the truth is that they have some character problems. The truth is that they're wounded, but not by me. They're probably doing the best they can, and we have a problem we need to work out." This is what we need to do when we know there's a difficult conversation ahead. Reframing and asking God to give you His perspective on the needed conversation will greatly affect the outcome of the conversation.

The Iceberg

Counselors often refer to "the iceberg." At the tip of the iceberg we see more easily the superficial issues of the problem at hand. What's more difficult to tag are the real core issues—the social or emotional life issues that are well below the surface of the water. As counselors, we work with and encourage clients to look below the water level and to eventually name their issues that continue to crop up in them and in their relationships with others. It might sound like this: "You've been teasing me a lot lately. But I sense that I've offended you in some way that has led to your teasing me. I feel there's something much deeper beneath the surface."

There can be—and probably are—several "somethings" going on! Don't assume that something is a "pure" problem. There are usually multiple issues below the surface. It's much more accurate to say, "Part of me feels this way, and part of me feels *this* way." We're not one-sided or only one flavor—none of us is strictly vanilla. Untangling and clarifying issues brings us to the base of the iceberg hidden well below the surface, where serious help can be given and received.

It's not profitable to deal only with surface issues, but that's a starting place. You might even want to keep this mental picture of an iceberg in your head and ask God to begin tagging some of what's below the surface. He's faithful to do that very thing. One major theme that keeps coming up at the base of some icebergs is a fear of abandonment. But if we've invited our Lord into our lives, He'll never abandon us. The verses in Joshua 1:5 and Hebrews 13:5 say, "I will never leave you nor forsake you" and should be found often in your Truth Chart if abandonment is an issue for you. That's where you're to camp and believe and walk in the truth. As you ask God to show you what he wants to uncover underneath your iceberg, don't be surprised at all by what He brings to the surface.

Like a good physician, He doesn't want anything to exist that you may have ignored over the years that it's time to address. He doesn't want you to live where your heart and your mind aren't connected. It may take some work, but that's what this is all about—getting to the core of what we believe and why.

Wounds from Corrections

When I was a youngster, the kitchen was a very unhappy place to be. I "never did anything right." For example, when I washed lettuce for my mother, I never seemed to be able to please her, and it was never done "the right way." She flew into rages. This happened many times and is the main reason I have worked very hard over the years not to injure others with my words. It's why I like to invite myself into a dialogue when I want to make suggestions or offer input, even if it's uncomfortable.

I would have loved to hear my mother say, "Sweetie, could I show you the way I like to wash lettuce? Then you can choose to do it however you want." I could have received that. Another variation might have been "Could I make a suggestion?" I appeal to you to really invite yourself into the conversation. When you choose to correct someone, you might want to pick the important battles. You can ask yourself, *What's the worst thing that can happen if I don't offer this suggestion? Does he [she] need this, or is this about me wanting to have things my way? Is this about my needing to control this situation? Is this necessary and appropriate? Is what I'm sharing going to negatively affect the relationship?*

For example, if your teenager is sensitive to suggestions and your suggestion could save only a few seconds in opening a can of soup, you may choose to remain silent. The higher choice is always not to damage the relationship. Trying to be helpful can sometimes destroy the relationship if it's not handled well.

Another point to consider is that in your area of strength there's often a downside. If you're good at something, and the people you're in relationship with don't have that same strength and you're trying to help them, strangely enough, it can feel bad to the other person. That feeling of unbalanced scales is their issue and not yours exactly, but to address the problem between you, you can say, "I can see that we might have a problem. Can we talk and resolve the feeling of discomfort between us?" or "I sense sometimes that you don't want my help, and that's okay; but if you ever do, please know that I would be delighted to help you."

Delaying Conversations

It isn't always necessary to have this conversation right in the moment. It's often better to have it at a later time when there is not as much tension and emotion. You can say, "Can we talk about what happened in the kitchen last night? What I want is for us to have a good relationship." If there is some resistance from the person you're trying to have the discussion with, he or she will be defensive. So if the person is inclined not to discuss it, you can go back to him or her later.

This may even give you time to think about what the real root problem is, not just the precipitating event. It wasn't about washing the lettuce. It was not about the can opener. It was much deeper. It might sound like this: "I sense that you don't want to talk about what happened yesterday; but if you ever do want to talk about it, I'd like to."

We have a responsibility not to ignore an unhealthy situation, even though we're picking our battles. We become a coercive person when we expect the person to dialogue with us when our major agenda is to get our point of view across *regardless.* We can invite the person to dialogue with us, but if he or she chooses not to, that's the person's choice. It does not mean that you can't share your observations of the situation.

I wish I had had the language years ago to address the situation with my mother. I could have said, "Mom, I need to talk about what happens in the kitchen when I don't do things your way. Help me to understand your anger and how we can resolve this ongoing problem." I wouldn't have been telling her what to do, but I wouldn't have been ignoring the verbal abuse. We needed to talk about it, the something dysfunctional going on, in a way that invites dialogue and agreement.

Not many people are going to run away from a conversation that begins with "Can we talk about how things can be better?" If your children's chores continue to be an issue, you can say, "I'm not talking about the chores being better. I'm talking about *us* and our working things out." In a parent-child relationship, there will be some negotiable issues and some nonnegotiable issues.

As children of all ages grow, they need to practice making some choices. Even if they don't do it well at first, they need to have that sense of ownership. Moreover, you become less controlling, and they don't perceive your leadership style as "my way or the highway." They see you as fair and open to suggestions. As they make choices, they have the opportunity to grow in responsibility and develop higher critical thinking skills. They also feel better about who they are.

It's a total winning strategy to let your children—of any age—have as much input on how things get done and see the consequences of their choices. A parent's job is to prepare children for their lives, and a part of preparing them for life is nurturing the responsibility that comes through chores. Helping them to take as much ownership as possible is wise.

Boundaries: My Job/Not My Job

I use the term "job" as something assigned or agreed upon in family or classroom meetings, another word for "rules." However, I encourage you also to think of it as an even broader term. When we want to talk to children or adults about a division of responsibility, we can say, "This is not my job—this is your job." We may even get mildly depressed when we feel so very responsible for so much. I encourage you to take it to the second column of truth and to think about what really is your responsibility and what is not. It's very liberating when you see you've taken false responsibility for something that God has not called you to take—and then let it go. It also imparts to children a stronger sense of what their role in the family is and helps you teach them about boundaries in the process.

Boundaries: Codependency, Enabling, and Caretaking

Years ago I came to a screeching halt with the shocking conclusion that I was a caretaker and not a caregiver. Yikes! Not only was I a codependent caretaker (not a good thing)—I was also an enabler! In my desire to care about others, I was actually hindering their growth by assuming too much responsibility for their problems, working harder in the relationship than they were, and wearing out personally and spiritually.

These behaviors all point to "poor boundary issues," but here's the story. If you have weak boundaries with others, you might as well picture yourself as either a doormat that has been trod upon or as a figure with tire tracks all over you. Get the picture? You've been run over—by choice.

Ask yourself this: in your care for others and for the relationship, have you given up who you are and your right to set limits, and have you done most of the "caring" in the relationship? If you're doing more than the other persons involved, you may be a party to unhealthy caretaking.

As stated earlier, I believe God has called us to be caregivers, not caretakers. Not only does the caretaker burn out and take too much responsibility in the relationship by mostly saying yes all the time, but also there's not enough responsibility left over for the other person in the relationship.

By always taking up the slack, you're enabling the other or others not to take on responsibility and possibly become codependent upon you and others who are willing to be caretakers. Years ago I heard a truth that codependents don't have relationships—they take hostages. This would explain the feeling we sometimes have when we're around someone who makes high demands on us, and it takes great effort to set boundaries with that person.

Here's a mental picture concerning boundaries: picture a stick figure on the left with few or no boundaries. Draw a doormat under this figure. This person always says yes. On the far right of this picture, draw a walled-off stick figure who always says no. She has too many boundaries. The wall represents her anger or even being too fragile, but the message is clear to those around this figure: don't even think about coming close. In the middle of these two extremes we put another stick figure with a dotted line around her. She has healthy boundaries. She sometimes says yes, and she sometimes says no. This is where you want to be. When your spirit is heavy and you begin to reframe, the truth about your situation may be that you've set poor boundaries.

Boundaries: Limits and Choices

Is it hard for you to say no? Is it possible that somewhere along your life path you developed an internal script that connected saying no with being mean? Another possibility is that you grew up under a lot of unloving control, and you long to be a little more loving, which translates to *permissive*. For example, do you have a hard time telling your young children no, when in truth they're the ones in charge in the household? That's not a pretty picture, is it? It is not a good situation or one that you can live with for long. Let's understand the reason for it.

Somewhere along the way you developed a message in your thinking that you felt it wasn't okay to set limits. As individuals, and especially as a parent, you must learn to say no when it's appropriate. Otherwise, you go back to being an enabler for people to get what they want out of you, and this isn't healthy for anyone. If you have a hard time setting limits and boundaries, here's a language technique to help you say no without feeling mean. This mental outline for expressing limits in a loving way to children is one that God gave me years ago. It sounds like this: "This [choice] is not okay, but you can do this [choice] or this [choice] instead."

Here's the story about how I learned this. I was scheduled to baby-sit for my then three-year-old granddaughter, Sarah, for the weekend, and my son, Bryan, said, "Mom, you teach other people boundaries, but you don't do boundaries with Sarah, and it makes it difficult for us later when you tell her yes all the time."

I said, "You're right. It's fun for a grandmother to say yes, but I'll try very hard to set some limits with Sarah this weekend and beyond."

So I began the weekend with "Sarah, you can't do this, but you can do this or that. Those are the choices." And again: "Sarah, you can't do this, but you can do this or that. Those are the choices." And again: "Sarah, you can't do this, but you can do this or that. Those are the choices."

Well, after a day or two, she had had it! She put her little hand out as I had done when saying my little spiel, and she said, "Nannie, these are the choices!" She had had it up to her eyeballs, was mimicking me perfectly, and she did get the message! It was funny at the time, but it was also startling that she could learn my new boundaries so quickly and successfully. I have shared that boundary-setting line with many parents and teachers since that day and have been told by them that the message worked as well with their children as it did with Sarah.

Being a Safe Person

For the most part, children respond well to parents who are continually working on the relationship and who are "safe" both emotionally and physically. Children are resistant to parents who wound them, preach to or lecture them, or attempt to control and change them. The choice of making yourself safe for others to talk with is what professional counselors are trained to model and purpose to do with their clients. They set up the counseling environment with whatever words or behaviors that are needed to cause the person to feel safe. The recipients of help must feel that they won't be attacked. Whatever the conversation is, the bottom line is that they know your heart.

You may want to give your children some language to help them feel as if they can approach you with concerns as well. Teach them "the sandwich" to use on you. I gave my children some language to correct me when they went off to college many years ago. This was about the time I realized that I was becoming like my mother in the area of too much control. I had focused on her control for so long that I was now repeating the pattern. I quickly went to them and said, "God has shown me that I have become controlling in these areas. This is not the person I want to be, and I'm so sorry. When I offer too much advice, or when you feel controlled in any way, can you please let me know? I want you to say, 'Mom, I'm hearing advice,' or whatever you wish to say."

They responded so sweetly. Thankfully, they never said that to me, but I gave them the language to correct me if they needed to, and this helped our relationship stay healthy and strong. I still invite their correction. It's called wisdom, good communication, healthy dialogue, and also damage control.

Besides control, there are other ways we wound one another and ourselves in the process. Let's take a look at some of these.

Shame and Blame Messages

Shame and blame messages keep you from being a safe person and will greatly wound others. Phrases such as "You never," "You always," "How many times have I told you?" and the classic "Shame on you" damage the listener and your relationship with the person. Maybe you've even repeated these words because they were said to you in your early life. We do repeat patterns—even the damaging patterns—of our past. It's always wise to re-pattern ourselves when we find ourselves repeating hurtful patterns of language or behavior.

The answer? We keep choosing better language. When we make mistakes before the new pattern is set, we say, "Oops—I'm sorry to have said such unloving words. That's not what I want to communicate to you. I'm so sorry. Will you forgive me? What I want to say is . . ." and you say it the right way. The simple intervention of correcting yourself is a wonderful act of humility. Each time you correct yourself is a deterrent to doing it again. Soon the words from our past will fade as we keep this new language close to our heads and hearts.

Fear and Control

Fear is usually one of the root problems of control—a fear of the unknown, fear of abandonment, fear of our children not making good choices, and so forth. When we're fearful, we grip even more tightly so there are no surprises, and then we become controlling! It's like realizing we're lost as we're driving along the highway, so we drive even faster!

In retrospect, in guessing the reason for my mother's controlling behaviors, I believe she had a great many anxiety issues. A first step is to pray, *God, show me what this fear is about.* Fear seldom resides in a person's heart alone. Multiple issues usually have lumped themselves together on top of fear. After the clarity comes and you name what else is going on, you'll want to reframe the fear. Part of the reframing process is seeing that when we fear, we're not trusting God for the part of our lives that feels out of control or is causing insecurity. Another truth is that continuing to fear is not helping us personally and is not helping our relationships.

Here's another peek at the possible dynamics of those who battle being controlling persons. Gifted leaders can run this risk. Highly responsible people can run this risk. Parents or spouses can inadvertently become controlling in the name of caring for their loved ones. When the caring comes with control, it hurts relationships and wounds hearts.

When you don't have answers for the difficult times in your relationship with your children, you can admit that you don't have the answers. What you're really doing is learning a "dance" for the two of you. You can say, "This is hard, and I don't know how to do this. Got any ideas? Let's think about this, and then let's talk. What I want is a good relationship, and I'd like us to come to an agreement that works for both of us."

Shopping trips with children of all ages can be difficult. But you can talk before the shopping trip and cover the expectations, limits, and choices the children will have. Even role-play with small children. By all means, role-play with teens! They'll soon learn the routine.

Honesty and Humility

Another characteristic to be on the lookout for is how you talk with your family and friends. Honesty is so huge when we dialogue with another friend or loved one. We don't have to have all of the answers. Again, when we feel we do have some input, we need to choose our words carefully so we don't appear to be a know-it-all or controlling. We can ask how we might help them. We can ask how they see us helping them. We can always say something like "I don't know what to say, and I may not be speaking out because I don't want to appear to be a controlling person in your life."

An example of this is a parent of an adult child who is a chronic overeater. The family was seeing a counselor together, but it was hard at home when the parents watched the over-eating episodes. In order to continue to shift the responsibility to the child and for the parents to not be in charge, I recommended they say something like "I don't want you to see us as being in control of your eating. Our job is not to be the food police. Our job is to love and support your efforts. It's your responsibility, but help us to know what we should do when we see you overeat. If we appear to be ignoring it, this is our effort to let you assume responsibility." You're talking about it, but you're not taking ownership of the problem.

What is your child's need—validation, attention, appreciation? An example of the flavor of sentences you can say to children with needs is "I sense that you have a special need to be appreciated. We all do. I'll ask God to help me be more sensitive to this need, because I do appreciate it when you put even one dish into the sink. And I do want to help build you

up, because you really are incredible." You're addressing wh.
the need is and using this as an opportunity to clear the air, t
make your relationship better, to make it safer, and to prepar
the way for your child to be able to dialogue with you mor
about this. It's a humble posture, and it meets his or her needs.
We don't want to miss any opportunity for our children's needs
to be met. You want always to be thinking about what could
be underneath the observed behaviors. You really want to go
below the layers. You may or may not be able to help, but one
of the ways you can help is to talk about it.

Our Messages

Many messages come to us from friends and loved ones
with veiled or even overt expectations. Examples: "I thought
you would call," "I miss hearing from you," or "I thought you
would come by today." Our answer can be something like "I
sense that you want me to do this, but I'm not always going
to be able to answer as quickly as you want me to. I'll answer
your calls [or I'll visit you] when I'm able." Or "I hear your
anger that I haven't done something you expected me to do,
but that's not something I could do." This lets the other person
know in a way that isn't harsh what you are and are not willing to do to meet his or her requests or expectations.

We also carry messages without realizing we're doing so.
For example, many parents stay with an anxious, fearful child
at his or her bedside every night—maybe even until the child
falls asleep. Some even let their small children spend the night
in their (the parents') bed. Many parents have shared that they
thought it was a loving thing to be the child's comfort.

But what's the implied message? Think with me for a
moment. This translates to a small child that *I have reason to*

be afraid. If there had not been anything to be afraid of, the parent wouldn't be sitting there or allowing the child to sleep with him or her.

In this instance, you must make sure the child knows that you believe he or she is safe. Pray before bedtime, asking God to care for the child as he or she sleeps in his or her own bed. It may take some time for adjustments, but your child will make progress, depending on your messages—those implied and spoken.

Where Are You Getting Your Love, Joy, and Peace?

We've talked about our controlling nature and areas to be on the alert in our dealings with our loved ones and friends. Now I want to talk more specifically about you!

Have you reframed some of your pain and discovered that you're letting other people rob you of your love, joy, and peace? Are you happy only if your circumstances are okay? Do you want to be okay *no matter what?*

I think many people fall into this type of thinking. I want to thank Sam and Mary Glynn Peeples of Birmingham, Alabama, for this input many years ago. They were studying Christian psychologist Henry Brandt's work at the time. The message they shared with me was that we unfortunately look to people, places, things, events, and circumstances for our love, joy, and peace. Moreover, they said that we often look to *creation* for what only our *Creator* can give us. I have thought about this concept for decades and agree wholeheartedly with it. How liberating these statements are!

When we look to others for our love, joy, and peace, we're expecting something from them that they're not able to give. They're to be "extra" blessings—but it's God to whom

we should look directly for our love, joy, and peace. John 15:5 says, "I am the vine, you are the branches; he who abides in Me and I in him, he bears much fruit."

Now let's look at what that fruit is that comes as a result of "hanging out with Him." Galatians 5:22-23 says that the fruit of the spirit is "love, joy, peace, patience, kindness, goodness, faithfulness, gentleness, self-control." It's not a grape at a time, either. It's the whole bunch of grapes. The even better news is that you and I can daily control the time we're enjoying God and our relationship with Him, whereas we can't control people. I ask God daily to be the Lord of my life and to fill me with His Spirit to the brim—as opposed to my being boss and the Spirit's being only oil residue in me.

People? I can't control them to give me pleasure, and I can't control them to avoid hurting me. So here's the choice: do we look to people, places, things, events, or circumstances—over whom we have no control—to make us happy? Or do we look to God, to whom we can go each and every hour or day and who has control over all things? It's no wonder we feel in bondage. We are in bondage when we look to these things over which we have no control to make us happy.

Perhaps you don't think you've ever looked to someone else to make you happy. Let me ask you a question. When someone didn't love you back, how did you feel? Were you robbed of some joy? Did it hurt? When certain circumstances didn't happen that you wanted to happen, did it rob you of a measure of your joy? If anything or anyone has robbed you of your joy—then you mistakenly were looking to that person, place, or thing for your love, joy, or peace.

My joy was robbed when I experienced hurt from my mother as a young girl and through my adult years. I let her actions and words to me become a barometer for how I felt about myself and my life. I'm urging you not to make the same mistake.

It's not okay for us to hurt one another, but we do it. It was not okay that my mother wounded me so many times. But the truth is that I allowed her to rob me of my joy. I looked to her for something she could not give me. I did seek God years later—after I could process the damage that was done—and was comforted by Him hundreds of times as I reframed my thinking. But I didn't instantly get that victory, and you won't either. Countering our thinking and behaviors does take time and will not change overnight. It is said that progress is a process and not an event.

God is a source of healing, but there's much you need to ask Him about before complete healing takes place. For instance, ask Him specific questions to make sure you're seeing the true issues. These might sound like *Lord, show me why my mother's approval mattered so much to me. What is it that I was looking to her for that I needed to look to you for? Lord, what is the truth about this wound? When did it start, and what do I need to think about when I feel this way? Lord, when others wound me today, help me remember that I can't control their hurting me, but I can control my own response. I can reframe the pain from it, and I can control whether or not I send hurtful messages to others. Help me see how I could even be wounding others.*

God has honestly taken the sting out of those days with my mother. Along with the promised grace I received, God began giving me the perspective that her verbal abuse and anger were her issues (the condition of her heart) more than they were about me. I kept asking God to show me the truth, and that's what liberated me. He was so faithful to begin taking off my blinders and showing me more about her needs. I was so focused on my hurt that it was hard to picture Mom's strong control and rage as places of weakness and fear.

Then came the truth—my mother suffered from anxiety. She was a people person, and she constantly put herself in social situations, but she was unsure of herself in those situations. What a double bind! Then, because of the fear that connected with the anxiety, she became controlling. Because of the disappointment, she became angry. I was a safe person for her to spew on. That doesn't make it right—but it was the reason. She knew I would continue to love her anyway, and I did. I learned to respond to her with words seasoned with grace. However, I did learn to protect my heart more with better boundaries over the years.

I learned from the wounds and pain not to repeat the same behaviors with my own children. I remain grateful even for the wounds because of what I learned. It's always the broken places where we learn so much. Most everything I have learned has been from failures and mistakes. For years I've wanted to make the most of my mistakes and failures. I've also wanted to help parents and singles not make the same mistakes I made.

I noticed for many years that children came to school day after day, repeating the same old behaviors—one of which was not knowing how to settle conflicts. I knew there had to be a way to re-pattern those old and destructive behaviors, and I began asking God to share His answer with me.

Children, from toddlers to teens, need some "language" to help them stand up to bullies in their school, community, or even in their own homes. A few years ago I developed a method to give them the words to use along with a place where this could happen.

I want to introduce you to a method that teaches children how to resolve their conflicts. I encourage you to embrace these principles as well and put them to work in your adult conflict resolution. The Peace Rug is widely used by teachers and counselors to help children work out their problems with each other.

Please go to the web site <www.peacerug.com>, read these stories, and learn how you can use the Peace Rug with the children in your life. On this site you'll find ordering information for the rug and additional instructions for adopting the Peace Rug into your life as a tool for better relationships.

MAKING IT 🔍 PERSONAL

1. A suggested prayer: *Lord, would you please help me look at my relationships from your point of view? Would you show me which ones need repair? Would you provide opportunities for me to be a safe person emotionally? Will you help me to be aware of the messages I give myself and others?*

2. Review the Reality Therapy questions. Complete these sentences, and write out the questions to help you remember them:

   What are you _____ ?

   What do you _____ ?

   Is what you are _____ ?

   What is a _____ ?

3. With whom might you need to have consensus this week? (Boss, coworker, student-teacher relationship, neighbor, family member?) What might you want to say? _____

   _____

   _____

   _____

   _____

4. Are you too quick to give advice, and is it possible it's hurting any of your relationships? Review how to give more thoughtful feedback, and write out what you might say differently:

_____

_____

_____

_____

_____

_____

5. Are you more aware of any ignored "elephants" (large issues) in your life? _____

   _____

   _____

   _____

6. What are the three things you should cover in your apol-
   ogy?
   I was _____.
   I am _____.
   Will you _____?

7. Think about whom you might need to write or call and
   share these messages.

8. Think about the last time you were offended by someone,
   that is, when they "bumped your cup." Reframe the issue
   that came out of the cup. For example, I felt _____

   _____

   _____

   _____

   _____

   _____

But the truth is

_____

_____

_____

_____

9. Think about something very difficult you need to say to someone. If you used the "sandwich" outline, it would sound like this: _____

_____

_____

_____

_____

10. Use the "iceberg" method, and ask the Lord to show you some of the issues under the surface. What do you sense Him saying to you? _____

_____

_____

_____

_____

11. Are you kind when making corrections? Are you inviting yourself in before giving feedback? Review the sentences given as examples.

12. Think about and purpose to delay your response to any difficult moments today. What might you need to do to help you do this? _____

_____

_____

_____

13. Concerning boundaries, ask yourself:

    Am I doing something that isn't my job?

    Am I unwisely taking too much responsibility in some of my relationships?

    Am I enabling or caretaking?

    Is it hard for me to say no?

14. _Lord, will you show me if I'm giving any shame and blame messages to myself and to others? Do I use "You never . . ." "You always . . ." or other shame and blame statements? What can I say instead?_ _____

    _____

    _____

    _____

15. _Lord, am I a controller? If so, what is it that I'm afraid of?_

    _____

    _____

    _____

    _____

16. The next time you lose your love, joy, or peace—would you be willing to process what it is you were looking to for those attributes instead of looking to God? Was it people, places, things, events, or circumstances?

PUTTING IT
INTO PRACTICE

You've had a lot of information to digest in the previous chapters.

Let's go back to some foundational truths we examined earlier about our heart and mind being connected. As you'll see in this chapter, Scripture says our thoughts and feelings are connected—and possibly are even the same thing. You can see what God has said about that connection in the scriptures that follow.

The heart, of course, is a muscle in the body. Feelings actually come from a part of the brain, and feelings tell us some important information about what's going on, such as "This is a wound; this makes me sad; this hurts," and so forth. The mind, or the more cognitive part of you, clarifies the information and hopefully leads you to a plan of action to help you help yourself or to help others.

If you were only *cognitive,* you would be void of feeling and not have as much compassion. If you were led by your feelings instead of choosing behaviors through a cognitive decision, you would be in a real mess. You can change your thinking—but not your feelings. Thus, you can have a little more choice on changes you long to make. So it's right to be led by your thinking, especially if you're asking God to direct your thinking.

Here are some Scripture verses that show that thoughts and feelings are connected:

O LORD, who may abide in Your tent? Who may dwell on Your holy hill? He who walks with integrity, and works righteousness, and speaks truth in his heart *(Psalm 14:1-2).*

Let the words of my mouth and the meditation of my heart be acceptable in Your sight *(Psalm 19:41).*

As he thinks within himself, so he is *(Proverbs 23:7).*

Watch over your heart with all diligence, for from it flow the springs of life *(Proverbs 4:23)*.

The word of God is living and active and sharper than any two-edged sword, and piercing as far as the division of soul and spirit, of both joints and marrow, and able to judge the thoughts and intents of the heart *(Hebrews 4:12)*.

The peace of God, which surpasses all comprehension, will guard your hearts and your minds in Christ Jesus *(Philippians 4:7)*.

Scripture also gives us the promise that God helps our dark or depressed thoughts. We're not left on our own to deal with these destructive thoughts from the enemy. We must remember that there is a way out—we aren't enslaved to our thinking. Truth liberates us to move beyond how we're feeling into what we know as truth.

God . . . comforts the depressed *(2 Corinthians 7:6)*.

Yes, God does comfort the depressed with His truth, and in light of this connection, we need more than ever to take a hard look at what messages we're giving ourselves. Sometimes those messages will seem like thoughts, and at other times they'll seem like feelings. Whatever the messages, they must line up with God's truth to make sure that we're walking in truth and not lies.

Behold, You desire truth in the innermost being, and in the hidden part You will make me know wisdom *(Psalm 51:6)*.

The following verses are a picture of Jesus' ministry and mission in your life; they've also been my life verses for years. They express my deep longing to help myself and others break free from damaging thoughts and brokenness as these things appear in the heart and mind. I long for you to be able to use these mental outlines to help rescue and restore your thoughts.

The Spirit of the Lord GOD is upon me, because the LORD has anointed me to bring good news to the afflicted; He has sent me to bind up the brokenhearted, To proclaim liberty to captives and freedom to prisoners . . . To comfort all who mourn . . . giving them a garland instead of ashes, The oil of gladness instead of mourning *(Isaiah 61:1-3).*

The goal is to do the mental work every time a difficult thought or feeling surfaces. It's often very hard work to catch these fleeting wounds and arrows, but soon your reaction time will get quicker and stronger. Soon it won't be necessary for you to write down your mental outline; you'll be able to picture it in your head. This is a secret weapon for you to take with you at all times. Go forth, fellow warriors!

Preach the word; be ready in season and out of season; reprove, rebuke, exhort, with great patience and instruction. For the time will come when they will not endure sound doctrine; but wanting to have their ears tickled, they will accumulate for themselves teachers in accordance with their own desires, and will turn away their ears from the truth and will turn aside to myths *(2 Timothy 4:2-4).*

These powerful verses remind us we have the choice of truth or myths. They speak to future times when we're going to need to endure sound doctrine, and I believe that's as much involved in our self-talk as in someone preaching the Word on a

Sunday morning. If you really want the mind of Christ and you really want Him infused in your life so that you'll live out sound doctrine, then you have to keep it in your head and heart.

The things that proceed out of the mouth come from the heart, and those defile the man. For out of the heart come even thoughts, murders, adulteries, fornications, thefts, false witness, slanders. These are the things which defile the man; but to eat with unwashed hands does not defile man *(Matthew 15:18-20)*.

These verses—as well as Proverbs 4:23—are what God gave me as the mental picture of the two bumped cups I shared earlier in the book. What spills out of each cup comes from inside that cup alone. Humans are fond of saying, "That person *made* me do that." No, you and I are completely responsible for what comes out of our mouths and what behaviors we choose, even when bumped by things such as circumstances or wounds from relationships with people or disappointments in life.

Earlier, in Matthew 15:17, we learn that what goes into the mouth passes into the stomach. The point is that what proceeds out of the mouth defiles, and not the dietary things. The personal messages we must give close attention to are the messages we give ourselves—self-talk—and what we say to others—other-talk. Sometimes the realization of this comes through a process that we learn about in Jeremiah.

See, I have appointed you this day over the nations and over the kingdoms, to pluck up and to break down, to destroy and to overthrow, to build and to plant *(Jeremiah 1:10)*.

This verse speaks to the principle that before building and planting, some plucking up, breaking down, destroying, and overthrowing must be done. In other words—before the fruitfulness is hard work. If you've ever planted a flowerbed, you know it takes a long time to prepare the soil. Often the hardest part is to pluck out all the weeds and remove the rocks.

This is the work you have before you to bring your thoughts captive. Some of the issues of the heart that come up are hard and uncomfortable to deal with. But if the weeds are taken out, the building and planting can occur, and that makes it all worthwhile! If you're going to look at your self-talk and other-talk, this tearing down and building up are an important step you dare not skip. Don't overlook the truth of what God is showing you.

> O LORD, who may abide in Your tent? Who may dwell on Your holy hill? He who walks with integrity, and works righteousness, And speaks truth in his heart *(Psalm 15:1-2).*

The last part of Psalm 15:5 says, "He who does these things will never be shaken." It matters that we speak truth in our hearts. Even the definition of integrity means that our hearts and our lives match—or are integrated. We are not conflicted. God wants you not to be overthrown. He wants you to be strong and powerful and not shaken. I have challenges and opportunities just about every day to be shaken. But if I can quickly line up my thinking with my internal Truth Chart, the answers and perspective come, and I'm no longer shaken.

> Is this not the fast which I choose, to loosen the bonds of wickedness, to undo the bands of the yoke, and

to let the oppressed go free and break every yoke? Is it not to divide your bread with the hungry and bring the homeless poor into the house; when you see the naked, to cover him; and not to hide yourself from your own flesh? Then your light will break out like the dawn, and your recovery will speedily spring forth; and your righteousness will go before you; the glory of the LORD will be your rear guard. Then you will call, and the LORD will answer; you will cry, and He will say, "Here I am." If you remove the yoke from your midst, the pointing of the finger and speaking wickedness, and if you give yourself to the hungry and satisfy the desire of the afflicted, then your light will rise in darkness and your gloom will become like midday. And the LORD will continually guide you, and satisfy your desire in scorched places, and give strength to your bones; and you will be like a watered garden, and like a spring of water whose waters do not fail. Those from among you will rebuild the ancient ruins; you will raise up the age-old foundations; and you will be called the repairer of the breach, the restorer of the streets in which to dwell (Isaiah 58:6-12).

As you continue to practice reframing, I hope you're in a healthier frame of mind to be the repairer of the breach. You're finding truth, and that brings life and liberty into your relationships. Language for friends and family will sound like "Could we spend some time figuring out ways we can be safer for each other and ways we can love more completely?" You're being courageous enough to talk about the barriers, and that's so huge. It's a tough decision at times to know what to ignore and what not to ignore about the behaviors of others. God can tell you best! It is tough being the repairer of the breach, because it requires so much work; but you're the most equipped. If God has burdened you and shown you the needs, He'll give you the grace and words to do what's your part.

A double-minded man [is] unstable in all his ways *(James 1:8).*

Do not be conformed to this world, but be transformed by the renewing of your mind, so that you may prove what the will of God is, that which is good and acceptable and perfect *(Romans 12:2).*

Attributes of God

Below are some entries for your right-hand column of truth. I encourage you to spend some time with the Lord and ask Him to show you more about who He is as you seek His perspective for your right-hand column thoughts. Spend time meditating on the truths of God and relating His attributes to your life.

- He is holy.
- He is majestic.
- He is good.
- He is wise.
- He is my truth.
- He is my true source of love.
- He is my true source of joy.
- He is my true source of peace.
- He is my wonderful counselor.
- He is trustworthy.
- He is the giver of my hopes and dreams.
- He is faithful.

- He is faithful to turn my present brokenness to good.
- He is faithful to shine His light on my wounds so that I am healed.
- He is my healer.
- He is beautiful.
- He is perfect.
- He is amazing.
- He is my rock.
- He is my adventure.
- He is my Creator.
- He is my future.
- He is my present.
- He is my strength.
- He is my safe place.
- He is my rescuer.
- He is my heart.
- He is the lover of my soul.
- He is my grace.
- He is my glory.
- He is the one on whom I depend.
- He was in my past, standing beside me each time I was wounded and hurt, waiting for me to ask for His touch and His grace.
- He is my salvation.
- He is my Lord.
- He is my answer for thirst.
- He is my Father.
- He is my intercessor.
- He is my advocate.
- He is my light.

- He is my warrior.
- He is my friend.
- He is my mercy.
- He is my justice.
- He is my deliverer.
- He is my freedom.
- He is my trustworthy king.
- He is my shepherd.
- He is my treasure.
- He is my tenderness.

Don't feel the need to rush through these powerful statements about your loving Savior, who longs to spend time with you and is jealous for your time. He longs to pour out His love to you. Spending time with Him and telling Him what you love about Him may be just what you need to make it through the day.

I've shared this with you in the hope that it would help you see the deep, deep love of the Father for you. It's the cry of His heart that none of us will be in bondage to ourselves or things in our lives. That is His perspective. We can't be truly free until we know Him and His freedom.

I invite you to stop and think about this and personalize this process before moving on. Think about putting your favorite phrases for Him in your own second column of life.

To the reader:

Although the main purpose of this book is to give you better messages for your own thought life and for relationships with others, I want to give you an opportunity to settle something else. If you're not certain that you've invited Christ into your life, you can do it right now. 1 John 5: 11-13 says, "The testimony is this, that God has given us eternal life, and this life is in His Son. He who has the Son has the life; he who does not have the Son of God does not have the life. These things I have written to you who believe in the name of the Son of God, so that you may know that you have eternal life."

I first heard this startling information when a young woman shared at a gathering in my city. First, she shared that God loved me and had a plan for my life. Her references for this bold statement were John 3:16 and John 10:10. John 3:16 tells us, "For God so loved the world that He gave His only Son, that whoever believes in Him shall not perish, but have eternal life." Jesus says in John 10:10, "I came that you may have life, and have it abundantly."

She shared a second premise that, yes, God had a plan for my life but that there was a problem. The problem was that the Bible says we're sinners, separated from God, and that I couldn't automatically know or experience God's plan for my life. Her reference was Romans 3:23, which says, "All have sinned and fall short of the glory of God," and another, Romans 6:23, that says, "The wages of sin is death [eternal separation from God]."

The third principle she shared was better news. She said that despite the sin problem, God had made provision in the person of Jesus Christ so that I could experience God's plan for my life. Jesus said in John 14:6, "I am the way, and the truth, and the life; no one comes to the Father but through Me."

The fourth and last principle she shared was where I had really missed the mark. Although I had had a heart for God and had attended church regularly and had believed the Bible facts, I didn't know that I had missed it! This was brand-new information. She said that it wasn't enough for me to *know* these things—she said that the Bible teaches that I must individually receive Jesus Christ as Savior and Lord before I could experience God's love and plan for my life. She read Revelation 3:20—"Behold, I stand at the door [of your heart] and knock; if any one hears My voice and opens the door, I will come in to him." I knew there had never been a time in my life when I had had this conversation with God, so I asked Him to come into my life that very moment. I prayed the prayer of invitation, and my life has never been the same.

Even if you have had a heart for God, even if you've believed facts about God and Jesus, even if you've tried to do good, or even if as a child you prayed some words or walked down the aisle at church, if you don't really remember inviting Jesus into your life before—you can do it now. These words I've given have no power; the power comes from the sincerity of your invitation.

Suggested prayer: *Jesus, today I realize that I have not settled or completed my relationship with you. Now, with understanding, I invite you into my life as my Savior and my Lord. Thank you for dying on the Cross for my sins and for forgiving me all my sins. Thank you that I have eternal life with you. Thank you that today is my spiritual birthday and that this is now settled. I give you control*

*of my life and ask for you to make me the kind of person you want
me to be. In Jesus' wonderful name I pray. Amen.*

If you prayed this prayer or something similar from
your heart, share this decision with someone special to you.
God's power, the very Spirit of God, the Holy Spirit, resides in
you, and you now have the capability to truly transform your
thoughts and to hear from Him.

May God bless you, and may you keep Him close to you
in your thoughts and prayers from this time forth.

MAKING IT 🔍 PERSONAL

1. A suggested prayer: *Lord, will you help me to see the connection between my thoughts and my heart? I believe that what I think matters. Will you help me to hear the messages I give myself?*

2. Think about selecting one of the verses I've given you in this chapter and committing it to memory. Write it here:

_____

_____

_____

_____

_____

_____

_____

_____

_____

_____

_____

_____

_____

_____

_____

_____

3. Select 10 of the attributes of God that you need to hide in your heart today. List them here:

_____

_____

_____

_____

_____

_____

_____

_____

_____

_____

4. If you prayed and invited Jesus Christ into your life as your Savior and Lord, record today's date as your "spiritual birthday:" _____

May the Lord continue to help you sort out the messages you give yourself and those you choose to give to others. Blessings to you!

BIBLIOGRAPHY

American Psychiatric Association Work Group on Eating Disorders. "Practice Guidelines for the Treatment of Patients with Eating Disorders." *American Journal of Psychiatry* 157 (2000): 1-39.

Anderson, Neil T., and Timothy M. Warner. *The Beginner's Guide to Spiritual Warfare.* Ventura, Calif.: Regal Books, 2000.

Bruce, B., and W. S. Agras. "Binge Eating in Females: A Population-based Investigation. *International Journal of Eating Disorders* 12 (1992): 365-73.

Clark, D. M., & C. G. Fairburn, ed. *Science and Practice of Cognitive Behavior Therapy.* New York: Oxford University Press, 1997.

Eldredge, John. *Waking the Dead.* Nashville: Thomas Nelson Publishers, 2003.

Glasser, William. *Choice Theory: A New Psychology of Personal Freedom.* San Francisco: HarperCollins Publisher, 1998.

Glasser, William. *Warning: Psychiatry May Be Hazardous to Your Mental Health.* San Francisco: HarperCollins Publishers, 2003.

Hastings, Jill H., and Marion H. Typpo. *An Elephant in the Living Room.* Center City, Minn.: Hazelden Publishing, 1984.

McIntosh, Helen B. *Eric, Jose, & the Peace Rug.* Dalton, Ga.: The Peace Rug Co., 2006.

Narrow, W. E. "One-year Prevalence of Depressive Disorders Among Adults 18 and Over in the U. S." National Institute of Mental Health ECA prospective data. Unpublished table. Population estimates based on U.S. Census estimated residential population age 18 and over on July 1, 1998.

Narrow, W. E., D. S. Rae, and D. A. Regier. "NIMH epidemiology note: Prevalence of Anxiety Disorders." One-year prevalence best estimates calculated from ECA and NCS data. Population estimates based on U.S. Census estimated residential population age 18 to 54 on July 1, 1998. Unpublished.

National Institutes of Health, NIH Publication No. 01-4584.

Spitzer, R. L, S. Yanovski, T. Wadden, et al. "Binge Eating Disorder: Its Further Validation in a Multisite Study." *International Journal of Eating Disorders* 13 (1993): 137-53.

Sullivan, P. F. "Mortality in Anorexia Nervosa." *American Journal of Psychiatry* 152 (1995): 1073-4.

Soli Deo Gloria.